Praise for *Silent Selling,*
Listening for the Sounds of Success

"Managers have to manage sellers yet few know how to pick winnable races for their sellers and few know that different selling skills are required for transactional vs. relational accounts. This book dissects the process in simple steps. This is a must read for anyone who manages sellers."

Dan Bennett, Vice President/Market Manager, Cumulus, Dallas/Fort Worth

"I've read dozens of books on selling and 'Silent Selling' is one of those books you go back to again and again. Mac Brand's emphasis on actionable activities and specific methodologies for achieving the results you want make his book stand head and shoulders above other sales skills books. His decades of experience as an extraordinarily successful sales professional and trainer are evident in every word, from his discussion of the limbic brain and its role in developing unconscious skills competence to his insightful listening and questioning techniques. I'll be quoting freely from 'Silent Selling' in my training programs."

Art Fox, Chief Instructional Designer, quickbizskills.com

"Mac's system enabled our selling teams to pursue potential customers that were the best fit for our capabilities and strategic direction. Mac's teachings in how to identify, understand, and manage the buying influences were critical in dramatically improving our success rate with large customers."

Craig Hettrich, Sr. Director, Sales, Nestle USA

"When first introduced to the sales philosophy, I immediately had negative thoughts regarding yet another thought-provoking 'learning experience.' Boy was I wrong! After shedding my old ways and understanding the true anatomy of a needs assessment meeting, I have since used the philosophy to determine if the customer fits my needs, not the other way around like we were all trained to do in 'the good old days.' The hardest part is retraining your brain to understand your customers needs and not make them need you and your product. Ultimately it is okay to walk away from a prospective customer, something the old me would never do. A true eye opening and life changing sales course..."

Marci Fechter, Sales Manager Southeast Region, f'REAL Foods

"Mac Brand's Silent Selling process elevated the competency of multiple sales staffs I led who benefited from his sales process evaluation and training. He worked with our customers to determine our true value proposition, which resulted in an improved sales process that was recognized and valued by our customers. This is a must read for all who sell or manage a sales team."

John J. Poulos, Founding Partner, DiscoverLink, Inc.

"'Silent Selling, Listening for the Sounds of Success' has changed my selling techniques. During our first work with, Mac suggested I put my laptop bag back in the car and would only need pen and paper. He emphasized that the 'customer will lead us to product.' Although skeptical, that is exactly what happened!"

David Willenborg, National Accounts Sales Manager, Bay Valley Foods, LLC.

"There are those who write books about sales theory and there are those of us who read them to obtain the silver bullet of sales. There is no silver bullet in sales success, but if you read 'Silent Selling', I am confident that you will learn about a sales process that when used consistently will definitely help you on your journey towards sales success. Mac is allowing us to continue on our journey of being students of our craft by writing 'Silent Selling' and sharing his sales expertise that he has practiced and taught with tremendous success."

Dimitra Rizzi, VP Sales, Farmer Bros. Co.

Silent Selling, Listening for the Sounds of Success

Published by Hugh Brand, Jr., April 2010

Edited by Mike Philips
Proofreading by Lisa Graessle
Cover Design by Gregory Borowski
Printed by Edwards Brothers Printing

Grateful acknowledgement to Harvard Business School Press and the Brooks Organization for their permission to use parts of their work.

ISBN Number 978-0-578-05464-3

To contact the author, send a message to mbrand@bellwetherfoodgroup.com

WITH LOVE AND AFFECTION FOR OLIVIA CARRADINE

Special thanks to the people who encouraged and helped out along the way on this journey — my wife Jennifer Spoonts, my brother Bill, and my cousin Gerald Jones.

A sincere thank you to my informal board of advisors — Art Fox, Rob Hardy, Alison Hulburt, Jon Jameson, John Poulos, and Sharon Olson.

Contents

Silent Selling, Listening for the Sounds of Success

Chapter 1
What to Expect and
How to use this Book

When I first conceived this book, my goal was to provide the sales professional and sales manager with something other than what is already available. The one gap that seemed to be missing – at least to me – was how to conduct the most effective *conversations* with customers and prospects, a technique I've been working on since 1998. My hope is that you learn from my experience and then find numerous ways to take advantage of it. But to do this you must first grant yourself permission to not act like a typical sales person. Typically, sales people spend a lot of time talking; trying to persuade a customer to buy what they have to offer. We're headed in the opposite direction.

You will learn tips and strategies from this book that can be used right away — that's my commitment to you. But within these pages lies a greater responsibility...and that's up to you. Think of this as our "upfront" contract.

You must ***practice.*** Only then will you become a more effective sales person and have more fun doing it.

After all, being in sales is supposed to be fun, right? We are the ones who bring business to life and get to actually connect with the customers.

If you embrace the concepts I set forth and learn to conduct the sales conversations as I suggest, you will have real conversations with people rather than trying to persuade them or constantly debate them. In the process, you will realize the many benefits that drew you to sales in the first place — independence, autonomy, relationships, money, and fun.

Your customers will enjoy and value their time with you and you will be more successful over time.

I have seen this process work with more than hundreds of sales professionals over the past 12 years on thousands of sales calls. I do not have a 100 percent success rate — not everybody "gets" the Silent Selling concept or wants to learn. Sometimes we're hired by senior management without buy-in from the sales managers which results in some resistance from the sales staff. However, about 80 percent of our clients do get it and it has worked for them. Most report a 15-30 percent improvement in their sales performance.

My hope is that this unique approach will benefit you, the reader, and that you will refer back to this work frequently, as I do with a number of well-written books designed for business professionals. I hope you are compelled to dogear pages or even tear some of them out to put them on your bulletin board. In short, the goal is that you learn something in every chapter that you can use right away, in your world, today.

Whether you use the Silent Selling model or another, you must track your work and progress. Many sales software and tracking programs are available, each with their own strengths and weaknesses. The key is to find one that fits your style and to use it consistently.

You will also want to continue to learn throughout your career. There are some outstanding, well-established sales protocols and programs available on bookshelves today. We use many of them in our work and I certainly will in this book. I encourage their use regularly. Some of my favorites include:

- *SPIN Selling*, Neil Rackham
- *Strategic Selling*, Miller-Heiman
- *Selling to VITO*, Anthony Perinello
- *Hope is Not A Strategy*, Rick Page
- *Influence Science and Practice*, Robert Cialdini

In addition to sales-specific tools, there are number of other important resources focused on the behavioral sciences — a connection you will come to understand in this book. The more you come to recognize human nature and people's tendencies, the better chance you have of forming meaningful and profitable relationships. Some important works include:

- *Sales and Marketing The Six Sigma Way,* Michael J. Webb
- *Primal Leadership,* Daniel Goleman, Richard Boyatzis, Annie McKee
- *Resonant Leadership,* Richard Boyatzis, Annie McKee
- *Power of a Positive No,* William Ury

If you invest in any of these books, you will quickly see that all are quite relevant to professional selling.

If you are foolish enough to think that you don't need to continue to work on your skills as a professional sales person or coach, then you are already in trouble. If you think that your company's competitive position, financial strength, your "better" product, history in the industry or established contacts are going to carry you forward in the twenty-first century, you are kidding yourself. This attitude is a recipe for mediocrity or outright failure.

Everybody Has Great Products

There was a time in the history of the business, not too long ago, where you may have had an advantage on pricing, features, capabilities, or distribution. Maybe you still do. If so, enjoy it now because, unless it is enforced by law, such as the distribution of beer and wine, it won't last for long. If you have a real product design advantage or exclusive access, then you are also in a very comfortable position. Yet don't get too comfortable. Whatever advantage you have probably won't last based on the trends and events in the business world over the past few years. But I am envious!

Over the past 15 years or so, the manufactured product differences have basically evaporated. Everyone has great products. As a sales professional you can no longer rely on your product, service, or organization to do the selling for you. You are now much more responsible for generating the revenue. To you, this means your ability to connect with what is important to the customer matters more than ever, as does your talent and the skills you bring to the process. This matters unless you only want to compete on price. If that is the case, you can quit reading now. I can't help you at all. You already know how to negotiate.

Setting the Stage for Success

The process outlined herein is solid and proven effective. Yet the words printed on these pages will not be the greatest value derived from this book. The true value will come from your ability to draw from the examples — by thinking about the principles as they apply to your own situations then *planning your own behaviors and actions* to move forward. As such, you must complete these three tasks, in this order:

- Develop and use a protocol, or process, that allows you to assess the insights you have toward a means for the sale, the relationship, and the true nature of the opportunity.
- Use strategies, tools, and techniques to plan the appropriate course of action based on your individual style, personality, and types of customers you work with.
- Use questions in a humble and curious fashion to move the conversation along.

One way to think about this is to use the Six Sigma principles for sales and marketing. If you are familiar with Six Sigma, you will recall these steps:

- Define
- Analyze
- Measure *then*
- Improve
- Control

If you skip the first three steps (as many do in a rush to close a sale), you can pretty much guarantee that "improving" and "controlling" will be a roll of the dice. In most cases, the diagnosis and the discipline of doing that work makes the final steps clear or, at least, provides additional focus to ensure you are working on the right issues — those issues that are most important to the customer. Think of it this way: A doctor carefully formulates a diagnosis before recommending a particular treatment, medication, or procedure.

Each chapter of this book will include real examples from my experiences as a sales person and a consultant over the course of my career. These are real events, although I do change some of the details in a few cases (location, names of customers, and places of business). You will learn what worked and what didn't. Each situation will be analyzed to define and measure what is actually happening from the prospect or customer perspective.

While I will provide detailed examples of this process in action, this approach must be performed in a way that reflects your own style and personality, in a way that sounds, looks, and feels natural. Otherwise, you will be uncomfortable and that will come across to the customers, making them anxious and unsure of your abilities.

If you are not prepared to work on your behaviors — before, during, and after customer meetings — you will have great difficulty improving or even staying relevant in the current and evolving sales environment.

It's OK to Not Know Everything

Many of us get defensive or even angry with ourselves when we make a mistake. Some of us even spend energy trying to rationalize ineffective behaviors. You've likely heard in the past:

"That's the way it's done here."
"The customer doesn't really know any better."
And my all time favorite, "I know it's not the best way but I have been doing it this way for such a long time that it's hard to change."

In most cases these self-fulfilling prophecies happen because we have never been given permission to *not* know the answer. And when you're spending energy justifying your actions and faking the truth it is very difficult to learn from successes and failures.

The reality is that, although painful, the lessons learned from mistakes are often greater than those from successes. Use that to your advantage, if for no other reason than you begin to minimize the chances of repeating the same mistakes. You have to go through that work and the only way to do that is by giving yourself permission to make the occasional slip-up.

Too many times, I have seen sales managers and sales people criticize each other and themselves for making an honest mistake. I like to call that the "belly flop." While wanton criticism is usually unproductive, the benefit of a couple of belly flops is that it hurts and, in some cases, is embarrassing. You get very focused on *not* doing it again.

5

You will find that many of the challenges discussed in this book overlap one another and the inherent hurdles you must overcome as a sales person vary little from industry to industry or product to product.

Throughout this book I will refer to a number of different sources, mostly in sales skill development and behavioral sciences. Many of the models and processes available today are very good. It is not my intention to replace or duplicate them.

You will also read numerous examples of how clients used personal situations to learn, understand, and, ultimately, embrace the process. My experience is that most people see the value of a new behavior or skill when it relates directly to something or someone in their personal life.

The key skill to Silent Selling, as you will learn, is the needs assessment interview — a technique wholly applicable in both business and an individual's personal life.

My sales process shares one trait with all others — the challenge is in being disciplined enough to use it regularly and not cut corners. Even at this stage in my career, I find myself occasionally tempted to skip steps. And whenever I do that, I almost always end up regretting it.

There are some traits and assets of successful sales people that are necessary regardless of the method being used. They are:

- Good gut instincts
- Experience
- Industry contacts
- People skills
- Genuine curiosity about the business and its customers

All of these are essential and must work together. I will address these in greater detail chapter four, Transitioning Sales Behavior.

Have Fun When You Are Learning

When I ask people why they pursued and stayed with a career in sales, one of the reasons almost everyone mentions is fun. Whether learning, teaching, or coaching these new skills and behaviors, it makes the learning process much more effective if you let people have fun with it.

There is another very important reason I encourage clients to have fun when working on new skills. In a relaxed environment, anxiety and tensions are lowered — meaning better attitudes, a more open learning environment (less reliance on legacy behaviors), and a better chance for absorption.

Remember that Silent Selling is no different than learning any new skill. It requires practice and diligence and involves some trial and error. The best sales people have fun with their jobs but they also work very hard at their craft. It's not one or the other.

Now let's get started.

Chapter 2
The Behavioral Sciences: Their Impact and Relevance to Selling

For most sales people and their managers, a more in-depth understanding of the behavioral sciences will come as new learning. It certainly was for me. However, you will find that much of this new insight is very logical and rational once you think it through — even if it doesn't appear that way at first. You don't need to worry about becoming an expert. I'm certainly not. But an awareness of some basics is very helpful.

Please note that I am not an expert in this field. For our purposes we will work with a broad definition of the behavioral sciences that include the work that psychologists and other cognitive scientists do to understand how humans interact, communicate, and process information. This includes reacting to environments, as well as verbal and nonverbal stimuli. As you might expect, some of this is hard science and some of it is less clear and very subject to individual interpretation.

This really gets interesting when one person, or group of people, wants another person, or group of people, to behave differently than they have in the past, such as purchasing a product they don't currently purchase or use or changing what they are using or from whom they are purchasing. Maintaining an existing relationship, while challenging at times, is a little less difficult — though rarely simple!

Well-known professionals have all written a number of best-selling books on the behavioral sciences, including the most famous, Daniel Goleman, who has worked with Richard Boyatzis and Annie McKee. All are highly respected in academia and throughout the business world.

I make it a point to buy any book this group publishes because I know I will always learn something useful. And I will draw from these texts to show you how human behavior helps shape the sales process.

A basic understanding of the behavioral sciences is truly essential for sales people in today's business world. Yet few sales people are even aware of the connection. It's time to change that.

First, understand these fundamental principles of behavioral science apply to everyone — you, your prospects, and your sales manager. Even a brief grounding in the foundations of the behavioral sciences will help you communicate more effectively, ultimately making you a better sales person.

But first, let's examine why understanding the behavioral sciences is necessary in the first place.

The Old-School Mind-Set

For those of us who have been in sales for a while, the concepts of "persuading" the customer or "demonstrating why we are the better choice" are commonplace, as is the notion of the ultimate skill of "closing." Like so many others, I firmly believed the sales person's pinnacle of success was becoming the ultimate "closer." That is until I began to realize that it was losing relevance in the modern world.

This approach was suitable when the vendor had more information and knowledge about their product or service than the customers. This was true for most industries until about the mid-1990s when laptop computers became commonplace and the Internet became accessible and easy to use. By the late 1990s critical business information was suddenly at everyone's fingertips. Today's customers no longer need to rely solely on sales people for information and insights and are quite aware of that fact.

I'm sure many of you have had conversations about "closing skills" with at least one manager, probably someone from the old school. In 1983 I took a two-day course on "closing skills." The focus was primarily on persuading customers or taking control of the conversation. And sometimes it worked — 25-30 years ago when customers relied on me for information and insights. No longer. In today's information age, don't even think about trying that with a business professional.

Certainly, if you are selling to consumers in a mass retail environment, (new cars or department stores) closing skills do matter and you probably shouldn't spend any more time reading this book until the entire culture of your industry or organization changes. If you are selling high-end fashion in a retail setting then keep reading. These principles apply in your business.

However, if you are selling in a complex environment dealing with learned graduates and senior executives and you think you are going to persuade them with facts and details, you are setting yourself up for a big disappointment.

Vendors and sales people must go beyond the traditional role of post-World-War-II-era sales. Customers today have a lot more information than ever before and don't really need you for as much information. What is really important to you is maintaining access to the decision makers so you can find out what is going on with them! That is a fundamental shift.

In the twenty-first century, the old-school sales approach has a few fundamental flaws. Among the most obvious is that this approach is ultimately focused on educating the customer or showing them how smart you are — behaviors that run the risk of offending or alienating hard-working, smart professionals.

It's All about the Customer

Neil Rackham, in his ground-breaking book *Spin Selling*, was the first person to start the discussion and begin to truly understand what made the best sales people so effective. Rackham, an Australian psychologist, was the first to observe and document that the best talkers were not the best sales people. The best sales people were those who asked the best questions and listened effectively.

Few, if any, potential clients are interested in your perspective or a "better way" as *someone else* defines it. When the conversation is more about how they define success or how to make your solution work in their organization, it is a much more compelling discussion — because then *it's about them*, not you.

Most people are interested in working and willing to work with an outsider who can help them with something important to them personally or professionally.

You can build a business case using metrics that are important to the customer. The important step, or set of steps, is to understand exactly what is important to that organization or group of people right now, as it relates to this set of decisions.

To get that insight, you must earn the right to ask the necessary questions — and that takes skill. The foundation of that skill is to understand some of the fundamental principles of the behavioral sciences and how it relates to human communication, learning, and information processing. These principles apply to you, your manager, and your customers.

Using Your Gut Instincts: The Amygdala

What's referred to as "gut instincts" comes from a very specific portion of your brain: the *Amygdala*.

The amygdala can best be described from this passage in *Primal Leadership* (Goleman, Boyatzis, and McKee 2004, 44): "*The brain won't inform us of these judgments with words; instead, the emotional brain activates circuitry that runs from the limbic centers into the gut, giving us the compelling sense that this feels right. The amygdala then lets us know its conclusions primarily through circuitry extending into the gastrointestinal tract that literally creates a gut feeling...implicit learning — that is, the lessons in life we pick up without being aware that we are learning them.*"

This validation has significant implications in a number of human endeavors and sales certainly falls into that group.

My first work with many clients is to get them to trust their gut instincts by understanding why they feel the way they do about a situation. This requires some new thinking and might be uncomfortable at first.

But the amygdala is not the only part of the brain that influences human behavior or sales.

The Neocortex

"*The neocortex governs analytical and technical ability. This part of the brain grasps quickly and can figure out from reading a book how to use a computer program or the basics of making a sales call (product features, benefits, pricing options, availability, competitive comparison). The neocortex operates with great efficiency, so long as it is learning technical or analytical skills."* (*Primal Leadership: Learning to Lead with Emotional Intelligence,* Goleman, Boyatzis, and McKee 2004, 102-105)

The Limbic Brain

"The limbic brain is a much slower learner, particularly when the challenge is to relearn deeply ingrained habits. This matters immensely when trying to improve leadership and many other skills (in my view sales skills fit in here). *At their most basic level, these skills come down to habits learned early in life and this certainly applies to natural sales ability, at least as many have always thought it to be. If these habits and behaviors are no longer effective and/or holding a person back, learning takes longer. It needs lots of practice and repetition.*

The task is doubled to undo habits that do not work any longer; therefore, motivation is crucial." (*Primal Leadership: Learning to Lead with Emotional Intelligence,* Goleman, Boyatzis, and McKee 2004, 102-105)

In laymen's terms, the neocortex is about knowing things and retaining information, if even for a short period of time (think back to college). The limbic brain, the behavioral driver, is about doing things and much more impacted by the emotional state. That is where the challenge gets interesting.

We are hardwired to make it difficult to change our instinctive, learned behaviors whose effectiveness has been seemingly validated over a lifetime of experience. For some, recognition that these behaviors need changing evokes a feeling of inadequacy or even failure, which is not true. The fact is that today we have new information not available 10-15 years ago.

Back in prehistoric, caveman days, before language, the printed word, or any type of formal communication, a well-developed limbic brain was essential to survival. Time-tested knowledge of how to gather food and how and under what conditions to protect yourself and other tribe members from any number of threats was the key tool for surviving in a harsh environment.

Fast forward to the twenty-first century of selling in the global, professional world of business and this survival tool can become an impediment to success. You might find yourself in a career suddenly faced with new, validated data that confirms some of the skills, habits, and techniques you have developed are out of date or in need of some significant retooling.

The fundamental challenge in learning new behaviors and related skills is that you can't learn them in the traditional classroom or workshop environment. The human brain — especially that of a sales person — needs real-world experience. Yet many companies spend hundreds of thousands of dollars on classroom training, expecting that this work will result in long-term behavioral changes in sales people. It won't. It never has.

If you are responsible for training a sales team at any level and the training curriculum does not include fieldwork with the sales people calling on real customers in their markets, you simply will not get results. Personally, I would be skeptical of any sales training organization that tries to demonstrate how great their programs are without field training and coaching. And, as a senior executive, don't be fooled into thinking that just because a team went through a training exercise it means their improvement is consistently sustained.

Effective skill-set development work involves the rigor and discipline of concrete, clear steps — thresholds, benchmarks, performance tracking, and coaching. Otherwise, it is one-time window dressing, set up so you can check the "training" box on your annual performance review.

For some, that can be a very disconcerting experience.

Get Rid of What Doesn't Work

This is a politically incorrect way of saying that you sometimes need to examine your own sales behaviors. You can no longer assume, or be complacent with, the way(s) you have always sold or what worked for you last month, last year, or even two years ago. Frankly, if you think and act like a typical sales person, that is exactly how you are going to get treated — which is not what you want, is it?

There are two fundamental issues on this subject — your skill as a sales person and your knowledge of the customers' business. The first is that you must continue to work on your game and skills while working on understanding the customer and industry issues. The reality is both — not an either or.

Your skills need fine-tuning, your strategy evolves subtlety over time, the customers' business and political pressures move and evolve — you need to stay on top of all that. About 20 years ago, my cousin, Gerald Jones, introduced me to this concept of being a student of your customers' business and a student of your sales craft — and he is right on. All of that matters. It matters mostly because it impacts your mind-set and priorities.

Gerald stated, "*I think the big issue is more than skill. It's an attitude...an attitude that is totally, sincerely, and deeply interested in 1). both your client (the person) and the client's business and 2). learning and growing yourself. I found, as but one of several examples in the research we did at Forum Corporation, that there was a direct correlation between an attitude about the customer (vs. one's product, one's presentation, one's quota) and the amount and quality of prep time, better questions (really being curious), better listening, etc...and then, success!!! And the better sales people (in the opinions of the client!) spent four times more on their own development.*"

Simply, you have to work on you *and* understanding your customers' business. Both matter and they matter a lot. That means understanding your customers' business is what gives you the ability and competence to talk to them about what matters to them first, which is how you get them engaged, versus talking only about your stuff which is only all about you. This is how you get those tough appointments and start developing those relationships that you want so badly — make it about the other person. This is what we are going to work on in the following chapters.

What many sales people struggle with the most is letting go of old, tired behaviors that simply don't work anymore. Your brain is simply not designed to do that. At first it will be counter-intuitive, which is why you have to practice so it becomes something you don't have to think about. It simply becomes a habit, the way you regularly do things.

As you read through this book, you will encounter examples and a list of questions at the end of some chapters. Try these steps to get started. You don't necessarily need to follow these to master the process. It is just one way I recommend based on my experience. Since we haven't met, I don't have a sense of your learning style so you will need to identify your own style, if you haven't already done so.

Re-learning behaviors or learning new behaviors requires that you do two things. First, you must allot time to learn the skills and practice them. Then the hard part starts. You must keep working on it but be patient with yourself. The average time line for learning these new behaviors is about 90 days.

Interestingly, in many organizations (including some of my own past employers), senior management was often the last part of the organization to understand the realities of the behavioral sciences in the modern business world. They always seemed to want a new product, a different organizational structure, or any number of other cosmetic changes that would temporarily mask the problems while failing to address the real, fundamental issues.

Setting the Emotional Tone

Human behavior is often dictated by communication, be it good or bad. And that communication usually is directly tied to an individual's emotional state at that particular time. If that state is thrown off, then the emotional connection does not occur. Therefore the communication is not nearly as effective. During any discussion, each person plays a role in setting the emotional tone. Some basic guidelines:

- Stop and listen!
- Experts tell us that 80 percent of communication is nonverbal, which makes senses if you think about. You can tell a lot about situation without anyone ever saying a word.
- So the nonverbal piece of the conversation outweighs the actual words being spoken by a ratio of four to one.
- Your emotional mind-set is a large driver of how you come across to the other person.
- Part of effective communication is the two parts of listening — actually listening — then proving to the other person that you heard them loud and clear.
- You have to prove to the other person that you are listening. If you feel pressured to say to the other person, "I'm listening," you

have lost 30-80 percent of the essential validation to the other person. The emotional connection is, therefore, not completed.

- As a sales person, you have much more power than you realize in setting the emotional tone in a customer meeting or relationship.
- You can move the direction and tone of the relationship. The challenge is being realistic about how far you can move it.

You have to prove to the other person that you are listening. If you feel the pressure to say to the other person, "I'm listening," you have lost between 30-80 percent of the essential validation to the other person. The emotional connection is, therefore, not completed.

Think about one set of life experiences to which any sales person can relate — the tone the boss sets, be it positive or negative. This matters in your personal life as well. The tone of any discussion with a close friend or loved one can significantly impact many behaviors and outcomes.

If you think about it, we watch our elected officials and senior executives very closely and can really sense what is going on with them. This is, of course, part of the reason many of these leaders try very hard to manage the message. If you are the sales manager or the leader of any organization, your actions matter more than the words you speak — the behaviors are what we watch and remember.

The same principles apply if they are excited about something and think it can be done — again we all watch the actions, the body language, their mood. We make our own assessment — do they really believe what they are saying or are they just going through the motions.

The same holds true during a sales conversation between a sales person and a client. You have more influence than you may realize about how the tone of a sales discussion progresses. If you focus on asking good questions that indicate a clear understanding of the customer's issues or perspective, you will get a much different set of responses than if you simply push your product or service.

You can use the emotional tone you have set to keep the conversation at a level that works for you based on how you read the customer. If the person does not, or cannot, respond in a way that works for you, you can confidently make the decision about how to move forward (or not at all) and with what level of investment based on the conversation and the resulting feedback — versus guessing as much.

My Experience

One of my sales managers, who later became a good friend, once said to me, "Mac, you are well thought of. But the question I always get asked is, 'Can he make the big sale?'" I ultimately did and he was the first to congratulate me.

Of course, getting that big sale had nothing to do with closing skills. It was more about finding out what was important to the key influencers in the organization which included:

- Who was going to be involved in making the decisions?
- How did they work together with other members of the staff?
- Who had the veto vote?
- What competitive pressures were they under?
- What competitive pressures was the other vendor under?
- What were the internal politics?

This required a significant investment in listening, fact finding, and detective work, then building the business case and putting together the right proposal. The other big ingredient was patience, especially the rigor and discipline of doing things that were inconvenient and didn't appear to have a direct relationship to whether or not the sale was going to happen. As you might imagine, I was often asked why I was spending so much time with the people in that organization and in their retail outlets.

During that time, it was interesting to learn that whenever I attempted to engage anyone at my corporate office about the politics of my potential client's organization, the reaction was always based on one of three approaches:

- *We have a better product. Tell them more about that.*
- *See what we can do on price.*
- *Let one of us talk to one of their senior executives. Maybe someone more senior from our side can move things along quicker.*

When I began to hear those types of comments, I was reminded that part of my responsibility was to manage my senior leadership team. I had to make sure they were comfortable, without giving them too much information, so I didn't make the mistake of spending too much time on some of the important issues they didn't seem to know or care about.

No one ever mentioned listening, building information pipelines, or networking. They certainly didn't talk about understanding or working to influence the emotional tone.

The reality is that by spending time with these clients, learning their emotional drivers, inner politics, and preferred styles of communication, I was able to set the emotional tone in a place that worked best for me and, ultimately, best for them. I invested in the relationship, listened, and found out what was important to *them* before making a push toward a sale.

The word at the home office was that I finally "closed the big one." Ironically, all the senior executives — who immediately began to take credit for the sale — had no idea how it had happened. How could they? They had not participated in more than one or two meetings, making only token appearances at that. Yet they were all suddenly experts on any number of subjects relating to that piece of business. (I am sure most of you have had this experience — success has many fathers, failure is an orphan.)

Remember: You are not just a sales person but also a relationship manager. Like the relationships you have in your personal life, they are all different and all require a different tone when effectively communicating.

Chapter 3
Transitioning Sales Behavior

Now we will begin to introduce some of the realities of common sales behaviors and examine why it is such hard work to change ineffective patterns. Then we will explain strategies on how to reverse these bad habits and become more effective sales people. However, the ability to transition behavior must first be driven by some greater goal or desire.

When we decide to change our behaviors, it is generally because we want a different result than the norm. When you think about the times you have fundamentally changed something, it is probably because you were unhappy with a situation or the results you had been getting.

You can't just decide yourself or tell someone who has been practicing an instinctive behavior for 10-20 years to just "stop doing that." This is a classic neocortex, limbic brain example and it will not work — a person's past behaviors have probably worked on some level, albeit poorly. So simply telling someone to eliminate a somewhat effective behavior will not make an impact. A methodic, complete transition is required.

You must first give yourself permission to get past the "I have always done it this way" mind-set and that takes time, particularly with the most tenured sales people. As a manager, you must be prepared for resistance from your sales team and understand that patience and determination is key.

When working on changing perpetual behaviors you must realize it is going to take time, for all the reasons mentioned in the chapter on behavioral sciences. My advice is to break it down into a few simple parts and work on them individually. For example, when you start working on learning the needs assessment process, find two or three questions you like then practice them in a safe environment (more on that in chapter five). Realize this is limbic brain territory, so practice, practice, practice — you *will* get there as long as you stick with it.

From my life experience, it takes about 90 days to change a habit. That is how long it took me to begin to lose 35 pounds about 30 years ago. I saw a picture of myself from a trade show and couldn't believe who that fat guy was! It was me! I immediately decided that was not who I was going to be, ever again. The decision was the easy part. Following through and sticking to my plan was much more challenging. And of course it took practice.

The Role of Self-Image and Why Most Sales Training Programs (and Diets) Fail

We can debate the science of diets that work and those that don't or why we have an obesity epidemic in America (and one getting underway in other developed nations). In my view, the reason that most diets fail is the same reason most sales skill development initiatives don't meet expectations — the majority of these programs fail to address the issue of the individual's self-image.

In the case of a diet, until the overweight person's self-image fundamentally changes, the diet won't be effective in the long term. The individual must ***think of themselves*** as in good physical condition, someone in control of what and how much they eat.

The same applies to sales skill development — if a sales person views themselves as simply a "product seller," they will behave accordingly. And when sales management encourages, coaches, and reinforces those one-dimensional and simplistic behaviors, the sales person will struggle to develop his or her own skills. You can really see this when interacting with a sales person who is only concerned with their product, category, and what they know. Generally speaking, that's about the extent of their professional range.

For a sales person, or any person, to transition behaviors and actions over time, the self-image must drive that process. The individual must view themselves as someone who is good at analyzing business opportunities, understanding customers' businesses, and setting priorities based on solid information. This is someone I refer to as the "networked industry consultant." When a sales professional begins thinking of themselves as a networked industry consultant — someone who really knows their industry patterns and trends and the big picture — and can truly act as a resource to their clients, customers, and prospects, the fundamental self-image transition is taking place and they are ready to learn new behaviors.

Learning these skills is a door that must be opened by the learner for it to be effective over time — it has to be about them and something they see as useful to their lives.

The reason that most diets fail is the same reason that most sales skill development initiatives don't meet expectations — the majority of these programs fail to address the issue of the individual's self-image and do not consider individual learning styles or patterns.

Sales People Simply Don't Like Planning and Analysis Work

Sales people generally don't focus on planning work for five reasons:

- It isn't much fun.
- They are not good at it.
- They have never seen it work very well.
- They never get any input on the criteria.
- Someone else judges it — usually someone who is not now or has ever been in sales.

If sales people worked with a planning and analysis system that was effective, the chances are much greater they would want to learn and master it. Don't underestimate the feeling of being judged or evaluated by reports, forms, and technology when the sales person's entire world is made up of people, relationships, customers, and markets. The execution of these systems is not a sales person's core competency (as opposed to their people skills) yet they feel they are being evaluated by it. It doesn't help that the companies who market and sell these electronic sales pipeline, process, and tracking systems sell them as "control tools."

When it comes to planning, setting priorities, and comprehensively analyzing a customer's business and the pressures within the organization, the fundamental challenge is that most sales people are not accustomed to, or experienced with, having collaborative, adult-to-adult discussions with their sales managers. In fact, most sales people will simply tell the boss or the authority figure whatever answers will end the conversation soonest. Then they hope they are never asked about it again. This is unproductive and undermines a productive relationship between sales people and their managers.

As the manager, the first thing to realize is that you must give sales people permission to not know everything and the leeway to work on learning new skills. By creating such an open learning environment, the sales person *and* manager can focus on what really matters — productive sales skill development. Having the support of a manager is also essential during the important trials of these new skills — sales calls with a manager are going to be much more successful if the sales person is focused on the customer versus selling their skills to the manager.

Arbitrary Priorities: Why Many Companies Miss Expectations

Historically, sales organizations have set the largest accounts as the only focus. The end result of this process is a relatively short list of accounts with the greatest potential return on investment. Many sales organizations and senior management teams become quickly frustrated with a low return on investment with their sales resources.

In working with our clients, it is always telling to ask a vice president of sales about their level of satisfaction with the return on investment and overall performance of the sales team and then ask the president of the organization the same question privately. The answers are usually quite different.

One of three patterns usually emerges:

- Sales teams have meetings with what seem to be the right people or accounts but have little or nothing to show for it.
- Organizations provide solutions that appear to match the customer's needs but they can't get to the right decision makers or they find the needs are no longer a priority.
- After much effort, the purchase decision seems to come down to price.

Qualifying and Setting Priorities

One of the most important steps toward becoming more successful in sales is to get very disciplined and process-oriented about setting priorities.

Let's look at some fundamental principles and behaviors that will provide a methodology to better set priorities using your personal insights, business experience, industry and customer knowledge, and individual style and personality. Keep in mind that *you* must decide what the priorities are — this guide simply provides an easy way to organize and analyze your thoughts so you get a better bang for your buck.

So many sales people focus on "closing the deal" or preparing for that big presentation rather than the necessary due diligence and analysis before reaching out to a prospective customer. I always encourage sales teams and managers to set priorities in a very rigorous and disciplined fashion. One of the ways we encourage this is to "go for the no." Specifically, when working with clients to set their own sales priorities, we develop tools and processes to first screen out opportunities with a low likelihood of success. **This does three things:**

- Reduces the expenditure of energy and resources on projects with a low chance of success so resources aren't wasted.
- Gives the sales person a better sense of focus, drive, and confidence — then they believe that the project they have chosen to invest in has been selected based on solid assessment criteria through the use of a disciplined process.
- The sales person's individual confidence increases and they feel empowered, in part because they have been given permission to say "no" to a poorly qualified opportunity or project.

Picking Winnable Races

These fundamental principles of qualifying and setting priorities apply universally and are devoid of context. It is near impossible to separate your mind, energy, drive, and overall sense of satisfaction in your personal life completely from your professional life and vice versa. Setting priorities is of critical importance in your personal *and* professional life.

It's unhealthy to work on projects with a low probability of success or those in which you have little faith. It is bad for your psyche and overall emotional outlook. In addition, you get a poor return on investment on the one resource every person on the planet has exactly the same amount of — time. Therefore, one of the elements of success in sales, or any other endeavor, is to not over invest in projects or people who do not fit what you value or desire.

Becoming more effective with setting priorities is as simple as getting better at picking winnable races. We practice this to improve our chances of investing the right amount of energy and other resources into each opportunity, in a consistent fashion. Usually, we have three distinct types of opportunities:

- **Clear-fits:** At one end you have opportunities that are strategic fits. They are extremely well-qualified. Invest in these aggressively and thoroughly.
- **Minimal or no energy:** Those worth only a small or relatively modest investment or no investment at all.
- **Not-so-clear:** These are opportunities somewhere in the middle of the pack. This is the most difficult group to understand and prioritize — how much investment is just the right amount?

Few sales people have trouble making a distinction between the two obvious groups — those that clearly fit and those that do not. What most sales people, and business people in general, struggle with is how to decide, in a systematic and consistent way, where opportunities and prospective customers should rank when the landscape is not as clear.

Qualifying

Qualifying isn't quitting. It is being smarter about how you invest your time, energy, and resources. This is simple but the popular saying prevails — "Simple is hard."

Let's talk about target lists first. Most sales people don't really think about what is on their lists — they just complete the forms so their boss doesn't bug them about it. If you are like me, I have had plenty of managers who loved forms and paper. And over the years, I became quite proficient at making the reports pretty and timely. Many were also mostly fiction because the sales manager rarely checked the work — he was more concerned with having paper! Yet if the manager is a good coach, uses the needs assessment and probing process, and understands their team members' learning styles and market dynamics, then these lists can be outstanding coaching and learning tools. But that is not the norm today.

The first difficult problem sales people struggle with is letting go of the opportunities that sound great in a sales meeting or a company social function but, in reality, are just not realistic. Letting go of these poorly qualified opportunities is a very difficult step for many to take.

The sales manager and senior management must allow the sales person to acknowledge that, as an organization, the company must be realistic about where the real opportunities exist and that the organization wants the sales team to work on winnable races. That is, working on prospects and projects that have a chance to be successful.

As a manager, realize that most people do not have much experience with really thinking these issues through strategically. Admittedly, some do but over 70-80 percent do not. Historically, sales people have focused on two things:

- Getting the order.
- Giving the manager the right answer versus really thinking these issues through, analyzing the data, or doing the pre-call protocol work.

Aligning Your Investment with the Reality of the Opportunity

Unfortunately, most sales organizations invest roughly the same amount of time and resources in each customer or prospect regardless of the potential profit or strategic value of the opportunity. Untold numbers of clients, customers, and organizations have an informal, almost instinctive, process for setting priorities which more closely resembles a tribal ritual than a business process. This can lead to tremendous amounts of confusion, wasted energy, and frustration.

This is often done without a methodical way to assess the viability of, or likelihood of, getting each piece of business and whether or not it would be profitable or really drive some other benefit, such as distribution for our employer. Based on our instincts of whether or not we believe we can, most of us go to one of three places:

- Get an appointment with a decision influencer.

- Sell something sooner rather than later.
- Work on an opportunity that at least appears to be a "big one" — one that has good marquis value.

We end up either under investing in well-qualified opportunities or over investing in poorly qualified opportunities. Of course, there are certainly going to be times when you go with your gut but those decisions should be the exception, not the rule or a regular practice.

Here is the problem:

If you can't measure it, you can't manage it nor can you diagnose patterns or trends and learn from success or failure. In a sales organization, everyone must use the same basic system or process for setting priorities and all must speak in the same language, vernacular, and protocol. Otherwise you will never consistently improve upon your successes or be able to take advantage of, or learn from, the experiences of others in the organization — whether those experiences are positive or negative.

What's in it for You?

There are two self-serving reasons to make a disciplined process of setting priorities:

- First, **you will feel much better** about those opportunities and projects you decide to focus on because you know they are well-defined and you have thought them through. When asked the inevitable question by a manager or colleague, "*Why are you working on that?*" or the opposite, "*Why aren't you working on this?*" you will have a solid answer in which you believe. (Of course, if you are using effective needs assessment questions with your manager, you won't ever have this type of discussion.)
- The second reason is **you will spend less time and energy managing the boss's expectations.** You already know the answer (and how you got to the answer) and so will your boss. You will not get frustrated or irritated as often because you won't need to answer questions about why you are working on certain prospects or opportunities because everyone is using the same system. **You will be more effective** because **you will feel better** about the support you are getting.

Getting Started with Setting Priorities

Start by asking yourself (or encouraging your sales team to ask) two questions:

- Given our capabilities, go-to-market strategies, and positioning in the marketplace, where can we win?
    - What are the characteristics and traits of the customers with whom we have the best chance to win? What do they "look" like? (*Who* they are comes later.)
- With what type of customers can we build a growing, profitable business?
    - Recap their characteristics and traits and any other applicable facets of their business.

At this initial stage of setting priorities, keep the discussion at the strategic level. I like to think about it as keeping the conversation at 40,000 feet so we don't get hung up in the details before we have clarified and defined the criteria.

The process of deciding where to focus is not complex. It is, however, extremely important and necessary — poor targeting will result in wasted resources with accounts where a sales person is not likely to be successful.

Creating Screening Criteria

The screening process involves the analysis of quantitative, qualitative, and logistical selection criteria regarding the opportunities customers might present.

By following a disciplined process that is reviewed periodically, you increase the chances of success with your target accounts. This comprehensive targeting and prioritization process is intended to create focus and a higher return on investment (ROI) by:

- Identifying prospective customers that match your capabilities and positioning in the marketplace.
- Providing greater value to key customers by targeting what is important to them.
- Identifying prospective customers that have a high potential for growth.

Screening Criteria: Strategic Fit, Accessibility, Size, Transactional or Relational Account, and Financial Health

You can use these five elements as a foundation. As you work with your process you may add elements that make sense at the time. It is up to you.

Each criteria will be assigned a score and will fall within a range. This is not intended to be an exact science, although the fundamental principles of using this approach are linked to Six Sigma. I like to use a range of 0-5 on each.

Strategic Fit

Determine the strategic fit of each account by identifying how well your company's objectives, needs, and business approaches match up with those of each targeted account. Consider the following:

- The prospect or customer's current distribution system. Can you leverage logistics or relationships?
- The relative importance of the product category to the customer and the customer's customers (internal or external).
- The likelihood that this business can drive category innovation or product line extensions.
- Compare the demographics/target users or business-to-business applications for each of the two organizations.
- The business segments in which the customer competes.

Accessibility

Consider the following:

- How effectively can you identify the right person in the organization and have meaningful dialogue with him or her?
- Who are the power players? What level of access do you have with these people?
- How well do you know the political environment of the customer and the change drivers? How fluid is that situation?
- How are decisions involving suppliers and their products made within the organization? How have they decided on these issues in the past? What decision-making patterns and trends have you seen previously with this organization?

- How well defined is the customer's decision-making process? Who in the customer organization has the veto vote?
- How much access do you have to the most important influencers? How well do you understand how these decisions are actually made?

Size of the Prize

It could easily be argued that the size of the prize should be the most important criteria. However, it is easy to be blinded by the size of the opportunity and miss critical elements of the customer's business model that may or may not make your company's go-to-market strategy a success. Consider the following fundamental quantitative metrics when evaluating the size of the prize:

- Overall profitability
- Operating efficiencies
- Margin contribution
- Volume
- Impact on the distribution system

Transactional or Relational Account

Is the customer focused on simply transacting business or do they value a relationship with your category of vendor? This depends greatly on how this customer views your category.

Transactional customers are those driven by operational excellence and primarily focus on price. They view most products as commodities and the supplier relationship is typically limited to the purchasing department.

Relational customers value the supplier relationship as well as price and service. These customers encourage broad interaction among multiple departments within their own organization and that of their suppliers and actively seek innovative ideas and suggestions. Note that some customers can be both types — relational in high-impact categories and transactional in low-impact categories.

To begin to understand if an account is transactional or relational in nature, start by asking yourself:

- Where are your relationships with this customer today?
  - Do you have access to senior management? Middle management? Or just purchasing?
- For this account, what type of relationship is best for your company? (This helps avoid the trap of providing a high level of service when the customer is actually transaction driven.)

Financial Health

It is arguably fairly easy to obtain financial data about prospective, or even existing, customers. Yet, surprisingly, sales people often neglect this step. If the company is publicly traded or has high industry visibility, it is quite simple to get a sense of their financial health, whether they pay their bills on time and how they treat their vendors. If it is a private firm, your industry network can provide pretty good insight on this point.

At Bellwether, we score these in a simple Excel format, scoring each element from 0-5. Here are some tips to remember:

- After the initial setup, spend no more than 10-15 minutes once a week going over your scores. This usually takes about 30 minutes.
- The real value is in tracking your scores over time. What you thought was a strong lead one day might not be in 30-60 days. Conversely, some opportunities you originally scored rather low might turn out to be better qualified after further work and investigation or when something changes in the market or with the customer.
- The purpose of this tool is to audit your own thinking — this is not an inspection tool to be used by your manager.
  - These scores come from your gut feelings (amygdala) about how a prospective opportunity ranks *in comparison* — **and nothing else** — to the rest of your pipeline.
- The scores are based on what else is going on in your set of prospective customers. There is no purpose in spending time defending or explaining it in relation to another set of accounts, market, or segment.

These Scores Will Ebb and Flow

I like to think of customer organizations and sales opportunities as living beings or a bottle of wine — they change with time — sometimes for the better and sometimes they spoil. To the sales person, that means these organizations and opportunities are subject to:

- Changes in an organization's political climate.
- Power brokers and struggles.
- Changes in the market.
- Adjustments as a company shrinks or expands.
- The individuals in management positions.
- Shifts in consumer markets.
- Geopolitical and economic factors.
- Numerous other factors.

As such, these scores are only a snapshot in time — they are very fluid. They can, and will, change so expect that.

For you, the sales person, that means keeping an eye out for changes in how decisions are made — who has the power, how they use that power, and what their priorities are. Admittedly, customers' organizational cultures will display a range of behaviors and patterns, from those that never seem to change to those that never seem to stop changing. My own experience has been that two things seem to always ring true:

- Fundamentally, few of these cultures change drastically over time. They may ebb and flow but most remain fairly consistent at their core.
- The most challenging to understand are not the ones that change frequently or never seem to change at all. The most challenging are the ones that are unpredictable, the ones in the middle of the spectrum.

As you get comfortable with this approach (limbic brain), you will come up with your own additional criteria as you fine-tune the tool to your world and customers. This will result in more efficient selection criteria, better focus on winnable races, and, ultimately, a higher return on investment of your time and emotional energy.

Chapter 4
The Needs Assessment Interview: Principals and Protocol

The most successful sales people share one essential skill – the ability to conduct an effective needs assessment interview. Of course, it also happens to be one skill successful people continue to practice during their entire careers.

When you become comfortable with conducting needs assessment interviews, you will see an immediate, positive change in your professional life and, most likely, your personal life too. Fundamentally, it is about having a business *conversation* with the other person versus taking the "information dump" or "persuasion" approach still so common today.

The needs assessment process is a mind-set and the path toward the truth. It provides insight and perspective about the reality of the specific opportunity in its current environment. It is also a significant fundamental shift from traditional or legacy sales skill development and training. And for many career sales people it might first seem counterintuitive.

However, mastering this skill and embracing it will enhance the context and quality of your business relationships. You will become proficient at listening to your customers and learning about their priorities — something every client and prospect values.

The needs assessment interview is one piece of an overall sales process, albeit a critical one. For our purposes, I will assume that you and your organization have some type of sales process in place that is already working reasonably well. If not, there are plenty of them available. You can certainly find one that fits your style, personality, and industry. We have a sales process at Bellwether Food Group that we would be happy to share with you. But you do need a process. Otherwise you will not be able to identify or understand what works and what doesn't work, nor when, how, or why it works. Beyond that, lack of a process makes it very difficult to track progress. My guess is you already know that.

You Are Already Good at Presenting Your Solutions

You know your products, their capabilities and advantages, and where your company excels. You are also probably quite adept at presenting your solutions to prospective or existing customers and tailoring these presentations to individual business conditions and customers' needs. This is not where most sales get off track — although that does happen.

What causes most sales proposals or presentations to falter is a poor or incomplete understanding of the *customer's* organization, politics, constraints, and priorities. As a result, the proposal misses the mark, addresses the wrong issues, or speaks to the wrong stakeholders.

The worst part is that you don't truly understand what you missed until the last steps of a typical sales process — either a presentation that didn't go well, an unaccepted proposal, or, my favorite, the prospect stops returning your phone calls. As a result, we tend to focus on the last bit of feedback or where we think we went wrong — usually the proposal or sales presentation. That might be the case. Most often, however, it is not.

Realistically, as an outsider, you need to understand the customer's world first, before a solution can even be proposed. This might sound obvious but many sales people and organizations overlook this important reality. If you get this part right, then putting together the right proposal or presentation is much easier.

The hard part for some sales people is realizing there are times when your solution — no matter how well thought out on your end — simply doesn't match the customer's needs. The needs assessment process will help make that determination much sooner so you don't waste time on "opportunities" with a low chance of success.

Making the Transition to a New Process

If you have been using a more traditional sales approach, such as "tell them how great we are," this transition can be challenging. Going back to chapter two, we're dealing with deep-seeded behavior patterns from the limbic brain.

For some, the needs assessment process can be liberating. Most sales people will prefer to have a deeper level of conversation with their customers and prospects and the needs assessment process facilitates this. For others, it is a much more difficult transition. But it's never as tough as you might think. Having encouragement and good coaching really helps, as does using this book.

The transition has been successful for many people, including the more than 300 I have personally coached over the past 12 years. It simply takes time and dedication to learn the process. And once sales people see the process is working, learning goes much faster.

Elements of the Needs Assessment Interview

The needs assessment interview is comprised of four basic elements, all designed to get to the true needs of your customer or prospect. They are:

- Spending time with your customer or prospect to understand their needs.
- Gathering as much information as possible to understand the presence of, or lack of, a legitimate chance of success at this time.
- Listening — not talking about your brand, company, solutions, or capabilities.
- Finding opportunities on which to capitalize in the future.

Strategy Behind the Conversation

The overarching strategy to this approach is to get the other person to think about and share what is on their mind — the truth. Only when you are addressing the right topic will your ideas be received in context. Otherwise, you run the risk of getting a negative reaction to:

- A perceived or actual sales pitch.
- Pressure to do something against their will.

- An expectation of doing something they are not qualified to do (selling up within the organization) or that could be politically risky to them.
- Products or solutions that don't fit with their organizational goals or culture.
- Something they don't understand.
- Something in which they simply aren't interested.

When you take a needs-based approach, one of the first things a customer or prospect will notice is that you are much different than the other sales people they have encountered. Your actions, including information gathering and genuine listening, demonstrate you are willing to invest in what is important to them. You become a potential resource, someone who is a listener and a problem solver, not an aggressive nuisance. By demonstrating your desire to understand their needs two things happen:

- You begin to find out the real issues and *their definition* of success.
- You start to gain insights for your own benefit and can determine very quickly how much energy and time to invest in this situation.

As noted earlier, part of the Silent Selling method and the needs assessment interview involves getting permission to ask questions. This demonstrates respect, allows you to set the tone and expectations for the discussion, and immediately lets the other person know you really intend to listen to them. Over time, you develop a relationship built on trust, which leads to the truth and what really matters to them. Then, and only then, can you build solid business opportunities if there is a match between what you can offer and what they need.

That also means that you never ignore symptoms or cues that something is not aligned with what a customer expects or ever quit listening and working to understand what is important to this customer or prospect today.

Given all the geopolitical, regulatory, and economic factors impacting the business world today, there is a real possibility of new developments or new players in the decision-making process. If you're not regularly assessing the needs of your customers, you might find yourself making an irrelevant presentation.

It is important to note that, whenever engaged with a prospect, be it an internal or external client or customer, you are **always** in the needs assessment frame of mind. Customers are not inanimate objects. They have emotions and will occasionally behave irrationally or unexpectedly. Staying in a needs assessment mode ensures you are always up to date on their current needs. This does not mean you don't eventually get to your message — of course you do. But you do it only after you have earned that right.

This reality affects every sales person. Even if it seems there are no new issues, changes, or other drama, this approach gets customers thinking and talking about what you want to know about — what is going on in their company.

Understanding Customer Needs

Customer needs are fairly simple. But they are often about an organization's culture and politics as much as they are about a product or solution. And the former factors often play a large part in the measurement of the latter. So a product might be measured both objectively and subjectively, based on those who manage the decision maker. Unfortunately, you don't get to influence that evaluation but you can use this knowledge to get a better grip on the opportunity.

In a business-to-business selling environment, customer needs generally fall into one of two categories — professional or personal.

Professional needs:

- Make money or save money.
- Improve efficiency.
- Recruit more customers or open a new opportunity.
- Retain existing customers.

Professional needs are relatively clear and can be measured in some form or fashion, usually with empirical data.

Political or personal needs:

- Improve political standing within the organization.
- Score points with the boss or an internal customer.
- Defend a previous decision.
- Deflect blame or get credit.
- Get more work done.

- Reduce stress.
- Get a raise, promotion, new assignment, or additional responsibilities.

While business objectives are easily measured, political and personal needs are, by contrast, very difficult to measure. But they are very important and every sales person must be aware of these decision-driving factors.

Almost every business decision has a political aspect, especially when it comes to outside vendors. Everyone has favorites, biases, and their own definition of the ideal solution. Whatever underlying opportunity, challenge, or issue is driving the customer's current behavior has a significant impact on how he or she will ultimately evaluate potential solutions. Of course, this can get really interesting when professional goals conflict with business goals.

As a sales person, you want to first focus on all the factors driving the need for a solution or a change then focus on how that decision will be made and who will participate in that process. Think about this is as a diagnosis. This means you must clearly understand the problem or opportunity *as the customer sees it,* before offering a solution. Even if you think you immediately have a great answer, the customer might not be ready for it yet.

Needs Assessment Interview Guidelines

The use of the word "interview" is important. Your goal is get the other person's perspective, what they know (or don't), how they see the situation, the role they will play (or not) in the actual decision making process, and what success "looks like" to them.

The mind-set you must have is one of gathering insight, perspective, and information versus persuasion or influence. Remember that 80 percent of communication is nonverbal, including body language and the emotional tone of the discussion. In conducting a needs assessment interview, use these guidelines:

- Make the discussion all about them.
- Begin with a long view then drill down based on where the customer takes you.
- Err on the side of wide-open questions.

- Take notes or pretend to (*bring the blank note pad and pen*).
- Use silence. If they pause after a question, that means they are thinking — don't interrupt that by talking.
- Follow your interpretations of the customer's answers.
- Never assume — ask if you do not understand something. It might be a critical decision factor.
- Use the 80-20 rule.
- Keep the discussion adult-to-adult.
- Stay on their level — not too fast, slick, or polished.

From these guidelines, the two I get asked about the most are keeping the discussion adult-to-adult and the 80-20 rule. Let's address those now.

Adult-to-Adult Conversations

Keeping the discussion adult-to-adult is critical. Many times, when a conversation with a customer or prospect is not going the way we want, our own actions and behaviors can quickly get off target as we begin to get frustrated.

In some cases, we will often try to please the other person, much as a child will try to illicit a desired response from a discerning adult. When this dynamic gets started, the goals for the meeting are quickly lost, as are both people's expectations for the meeting.

The conversation can go off track in at least two ways:

- Friction develops. In the process of trying to get your point across, you run the risk of engaging in a mild (or heated) debate. This is detrimental to gaining trust or establishing a collaborative mind-set.
  - You now might slip into talking to them as somehow intellectually inferior, simply uninformed, or, worse, ignorant.
  - Now you are in danger of talking to them in an adult-child fashion with you as the adult. This mind-set affects your tone of voice, body language, and facial expressions — all key nonverbal communication elements.
- The customer seems disengaged, uninterested, or otherwise does not give the response you were expecting.

○ In an effort to try to please the other person, you become the child. You risk losing your dignity, composure, and sense of self-worth. Ultimately, you still don't please the customer and they lose confidence in your abilities.

In both cases, someone leaves the conversation unhappy. This is not a strategy for a healthy business conversation. It's a recipe for disaster.

As the sales person, you have a much greater influence on the emotional tone of a customer meeting than you might realize but you must set clear goals, have solid protocol, and operate within your own professional standards. If you feel the meeting is not going well, then bring that to the attention of your customer. You can start that discussion with:

"I am getting the feeling that somehow we are on different agendas or out of sync. Is there something I should know about or maybe overlooked?"

The 80-20 Rule

When we hear about the 80-20 rule, most think of Italian economist's Vilfredo Pareto's *Pareto Principle,* formulated to describe the distribution of individual wealth in 1940's Italy. In short, it states that 80 percent of the wealth was controlled by 20 percent of the people. Many of us find the same in business today — 80 percent of our success comes from 20 percent of our leads and customers.

For our purposes, we borrow that thinking and use it to understand the role of the senses in effective selling. If you analyze the human communication system it is comprised of five elements:

- Two eyes
- Two ears
- One mouth

Four tools (80 percent) capture information and one (20 percent) transmits information. What message do you think the designer of this system was suggesting about how it should be used for the best results?

The 80-20 rule is an effective way to think about conducting needs assessment interviews. You want the customer to do 80 percent of the talking and limit yourself to 20 percent. If you can stay within that threshold, most of the time you will get the insight you need in the first meeting to easily determine what to do and, more importantly, what not to do next.

Therefore, to embrace a focus on listening skills, one could argue, is as simple as using your natural tools consistent with the way the human communication system was designed — 80-20.

Setting the Emotional Tone

In sales, as in any leadership or management role, the leader of an organization or the facilitator of the discussion plays a significant role in setting the emotional tone.

The most powerful driver of the emotional tone of any meeting is behavior — something the customer is going to be watching more than you realize. In addition, the emotional tone will affect how your customer appears to their supervisor, who might be the ultimate decision maker.

The best example is the difference between the two ways members of an organization form opinions about senior management:

- The *behaviors* observed of senior management by the members of an organization compared to...
- ...the written or verbal communications from senior management.

The team members of an organization may or may not read the e-mails, web site updates, or internal communications bulletins from senior management. Yet, you can be sure everyone watches the *behavior* of and knows much about the *actions* of managers and senior executives.

The vast majority of customers will respond favorably to a needs assessment approach, some more so than others. But all of them will sense if you are nervous or pushy and it may impact the way they perceive you. By keeping the conversation about them and not you, you are working in a much safer, more controlled environment.

What to Expect

You will find that many customers simply are not accustomed to actually having a person really listen to them. I have heard the same from my clients who have teenagers or communication challenges with their spouse. In fact, it is in those clients' personal lives where they often first see the value and effectiveness of using needs assessment as a regular practice. Almost immediately, they see a change in the nature and tone of their conversations with close friends, spouses, children, siblings, or parents. They also gain insights, candor, and an enhanced understanding of the other person that, in most cases, improves communications and relationships for all concerned.

The key is to really listen and prove that you are listening. That can be accomplished by:

- Not interrupting or jumping in with a solution.
- Summarizing and clarifying what you have heard.
- Taking notes when appropriate.
- Using silence to let the other person process what they have heard.

We don't spend much time honing listening skills as a culture. Whenever you hear a reference to someone's "communication skills" it usually refers to outbound communications – how good the person is at speaking or writing. Rarely do we think of communication as encompassing listening skills or observing the other person's body language. Certainly, we give it lip service and might say the words "I'm listening," but how often does someone actually listen to you?

But listening is a powerful skill that can have major implications to a sales strategy. Immediately, you can expect to notice some differences from a typical sales call.

- Customers will be more receptive to you.
- You will identify opportunities that did not exist before.
- You will realize some existing opportunities are not a good fit.
- You will learn much more about each customer, faster.

To get these results, you must:

- Get better with good questions (this will improve over time).
- Use more silence.
- Work at effectively summarizing what you are hearing from customers and prospects.
- Ask them for help using questions or comments such as:
  - *Do I have this right?*
  - *Anything else?*
  - *What else?*
  - *What haven't I asked about that I should have asked you about?*

When you ask the customer or prospect for help, clarity, or more details — provided you are sincere and they sense that — they will help you almost every time.

The most important point to remember in this conversation is that you can't behave like a typical sales person focused only on what is important to you. Your focus and behavior must be on truly understanding the other person's needs, issues, priorities, and concerns. When they see that you really are interested is when the information flow begins.

You will get more insight from customers as you become more effective at conducting effective needs assessment interviews. It is really that simple. And, you will make more money and have more fun.

Surprise! Most customers or prospects will make time for a discussion they enjoy or gain some value from — and that depends greatly on whether or not someone is listening to them!

When I hear a marketing person or senior manager who hasn't talked to many customers say, "Our customers don't have time to talk with our sales people," I feel like that is a coded message that really means, "The customers get little to no value from talking with our sales people."

One more surprise (this one is for the sales manager) — if you want to increase the number and quality of sales calls your people make in one day or one week, a great first step is to begin a transition from the information dump/persuasion model to the needs assessment approach. Your prospects and customers will be more receptive to meeting with your sales team and your sales team will have more fun meeting with customers. Everyone's morale will be boosted and your sales people will be more productive.

Becoming Proficient with Needs Assessment Interviews

This is when the fun begins. Your needs assessment laboratory is your world. Pick someone — a spouse, your child, a long-time friend, a barista at Starbucks, a wait-staff person at a restaurant, your next-door neighbor — it doesn't matter. The key is to start learning by practicing in a low-risk environment.

The first exercise is a contest of sorts. You want to get that person to tell you as much about them as you possibly can without telling them anything about you.

You will be amazed what people will tell you about themselves when they feel you are really listening, genuinely interested, and not working to use what they tell you to persuade them in any way.

Getting Started

The process is simple. Start the conversation with three open-ended questions about the other person — these are questions that cannot be answered with a simple "yes" or "no." Notice that each question is intended to discover truths about that person and what is important to them. After each question, employ silence.

- Sample questions for a child:
    - *What is your favorite subject at school? What do you like about it?*
    - *What is your least favorite subject at school? What don't you like about it?*
    - *What is one class that you can't see any reason for taking and why?*
    - *What is one class you would like to take that your school doesn't offer and why?*
    - *If you could tell the principal of your school to change one thing to make the experience better for the students, what would that be?*
    - *How would that benefit you and other students?*

- Sample questions for a Starbucks barista:
    - *What are all those ornaments on your hat?*
    - *What do they all mean and how did you earn them?*
    - *What is the funniest customer story you have heard recently?*
    - *What is the one Starbucks product I should try that most people don't know about?*

- Sample questions for a stranger at a dinner party:
    - *If I was the vacation genie and you could have a two-week, all-expense-paid vacation anywhere in the world, what would you do?*
        - *Where would you go?*
        - *Who would you go with and why?*
    - Since you are at a dinner party already, start with this premise — you can invite any 12 people in the world who are alive today to a dinner party and they will agree to come.

43

- *Who would you invite?*
- *Why?*
- *Where would the dinner be?*
- *What would be on the menu?*
- *What would you serve to drink?*
- *What would you talk about?*

- Sample questions for a business conversation:

  - *If we were having a discussion one year from today and you were really happy with how the year had gone professionally, how would that conversation go?*
  - *What would you be telling me about?*
  - *What is the one opportunity in your organization that only you see as relevant or important?*

On the surface, some of these questions might not seem to offer much insight into a person or their true beliefs, habits, or values. But as you continue to practice listening and tune your ears to their responses, you will see that you are learning a great deal.

After the other person has told you two or three things, summarize what you have heard like this:

  - *So what I am hearing from you so far, just to make sure I have it right is…Do I have that right?*
  - *Then, "OK, anything else?" and then they will start talking again.*

Do not jump in yet with an answer or a solution. It is too soon! Remember, the goal is to get them to tell you as much as possible and if you jump in here, you will throw them off course. Ask these questions (or some form of them) at least two or three times.

You will be amazed at how much people will tell you, provided you are genuinely interested in what they have to say. Of course, there will be those who won't ever open up or are simply not comfortable enough with themselves to be candid and open with you.

However, you will have the satisfaction of knowing that you learned more than most people do about those individuals and you can then decide for yourself if those people are worth your investment of time and energy.

The most underutilized secret weapon in conducting needs assessment interviews is taking notes. Here's the secret: If you are truly listening and focused on taking notes, then you won't be talking or trying to think of a response. As a result, the other person will keep talking as you are writing down your notes. To fill the occasional silence, they keep telling you more.

We will wrap up this chapter with a look at some specific needs assessment questions as they pertain to a sales situation. As you begin to look at these questions, I recommend developing your own and tailoring them to your own style, personality, industry, customers, and the world in which you live and work. And you must practice these questions. They must sound like you, and only you. — not something you read in a book or learned in a workshop.

Oftentimes, when we have this discussion in a workshop, at least one person will express concern over how they can apply this approach and not lose their style or other techniques that have worked for them over the course of their career.

One way to think about applying these principles is to think about the protocol and procedures for airline pilots. They must follow approved federal and airline rules and guidelines but within those guidelines they have tremendous flexibility and authority. For example, the pilots must follow the directions of the control tower. Yet, if they don't think the weather is right, see a gauge that doesn't look like it is within the appropriate range, or the flight attendant reports an unruly passenger, the pilots have the authority to change the flight plan or go back to the gate — it is their decision. They have full discretion and authority to make that call within the framework of strict protocol.

Cheating Is Encouraged!

I strongly encourage cheating so don't be shy about writing these questions down and taking them with you on a sales call today or tomorrow.

Permission Questions:

- *May I ask you some questions about your business?*
- *Do you mind if I take some notes?*

Broad Questions:

- *What is the goal of your operation or department?*
- *What is it like to manage a complex department?*
- *What pressures are you under that I might not see?*
- *In thinking about what you are trying to accomplish, could you help me better understand the two or three most important issues you need to address?*

Probing Questions:

- *Could you help me understand more about...?*
- *Really, how so?*
- *Would you be willing to share with me?*
- *You mentioned... How much of a problem is that?*
- *What are the implications of that? Who else is affected by that and how do they compensate for it?*

Digging into an Issue:

- *Could you help me understand more about that and some of the pressures or related issues that I might not see?*
- *What would a solution look like? How could we work together?*
- *If we could solve or improve your issue, how would that benefit you?*
- *As I recall, we talked about... Has your view of that changed at all since we last spoke? How so?*

New Product/Supplier Questions:

- *What do I need to know about how supplier decisions are made?*
- *Could you help me understand the timing of new product decisions?*
- *What could we learn from some of the best vendors you have worked with?*
- *What are some examples of how you have partnered with other vendors?*
- *What are the one or two opportunities you would like to work around that you do not have time to work on and/or wish a good vendor could help you with?*
- *How would we know if we were successful?*
- *When you think about a time you have used a manufacturer's brand/added a new menu item/changed vendors, how have you come to the decision in the past? Or, what factors might influence your decision to use a manufacturer's brand or select a particular vendor?*

Organizational Questions:

- *What departments or people could I learn from and should contact?*
- *How would you describe their style?*

- *How should I go about contacting them?*
- *What advice would you share with me on how to approach that person?*
- *What are the issues that this person might be dealing with that I might not know about?*
- *What else do I need to know and understand?*
- *Would you mind if I stayed in touch with you, to let you know how those meetings go?*

Summarizing Questions:

- *As we wrap up here, may we review what I heard from you to make sure I have it right?*
- *Do I have this right?*
- *Anything else?*
- *When would be a good time to get back with you?*
- *Is it OK to call you if I have any additional questions?*
- *You have given me a lot to think about — would it be alright with you if I took some time to digest it all, do some additional work, and then get back to you?*

These questions are just a starting point for your needs assessment interviews. They will be helpful in any situation, but remember to tailor them when you are feeling comfortable with the process. Put your questions in the context of your industry and ask them in your voice and style.

So start your list or cheat sheet right now. By the way, it is perfectly fine to go into a sales call with a list of questions. It shows preparation and you can stop to look at your notes any time – just ask a permission question. One good one might be:

- *Would you mind if I took a few seconds to quickly review the list of questions I wanted to ask you today? I hope you don't mind that I wrote them down so I didn't forget anything?*

You now have some new tools and a different way to think about a sales call so go out and practice on friends, family, and the Starbucks barista — then try the approach in a low-risk customer environment.

Chapter 5
Phases of a Needs Assessment Interview: Sincerity, Venting, Truth

"Unless you get people to lower their mental/emotional defenses and let you in, you cannot move forward towards a sale." (The Universal Sales Truths, Bill Brooks 2002)

The concept of sincerity, venting, and truth first became evident while making sales calls one day in the summer of 2005 with a client in Chicago. Our original intent that day was to show a new sales manager how well the needs assessment approach works. The three of us (the client training person, the sales manager, and I) agreed we would let the customers simply talk to us, even yell at us in one case, for as long as they would keep speaking.

To the sales manager's surprise, the shortest interview was more than 30 minutes long. All of the meetings were cold calls — not one appointment — and most we were meeting for the first time.

As the meetings progressed, we observed that not only would most people keep talking for much longer than we anticipated, but also that prospective customers went through what we later figured out to be three distinct phases — sincerity, venting, and truth.

We identified these phases following a series of needs assessment interviews with a wide range of customers and clients over the past four years or so. The more I paid attention, the more apparent these patterns became.

Understanding and being able to work with these patterns is an essential skill. Otherwise you risk ending the conversation before you get to the really keen insights. Worse yet, failure to understand any of these phases can lead to poorly defined solutions simply because you didn't have all the right information in the right context.

Stop and Listen

Communicating to your audience that you are listening is the most critical part of the process. If you fail to confirm to the other person that they truly matter — even just for a short period of time — then you aren't as engaged as you need to be. It doesn't matter if you think you are listening. *The other person has to believe you.*

No matter what you say to another person, the visual cues matter as well, such as looking attentive, sitting still, gently nodding, and making eye contact. Remember, 80 percent of human communication is nonverbal.

Listening and demonstrating that you are listening is critical to getting through these three phases. In fact, neither sincerity, nor venting, nor truth can be achieved without first truly listening to your customer.

And make no mistake — the other person senses if you appear to be engaged in what is important to them. If you are a sales person, this gives you an immediate competitive advantage because simply listening takes more time than most are willing to invest. You have a much better chance of getting the depth and clarity that others will not.

Now that you're ready to listen, use this skill to open the door to the following three phases of the needs assessment process that every prospect can be expected to follow.

Sincerity

This is the first phase when the other person is thinking subconsciously that this discussion is going to be like most other sales conversations based on their own life experience. (*When is the pitch coming?*)

They are expecting the interruptions and, at this point, not even considering the possibility that you are going to listen to them. That's because few other sales people do.

On a sales call, this is when you get cost questions or some other behavior or tactic designed to end the conversation. This is a version of the flight or fight syndrome — bodily changes and behaviors designed to minimize the perceived threat, which in this case is sales pressure.

Prospects want to be able to say they met with you and have future access to you but don't really expect much more from you than that you try to persuade or influence them.

When you offer unsolicited advice before the other person is ready for it, regardless of how much of an expert you are, that behavior sends a clear message that you are thinking only about what you want. A logical conclusion for the other person is that you couldn't possibly understand their needs — you have just proven that you aren't listening.

This sincerity phase is the most critical as this is when the defense mechanisms begin to loosen up. Expect about 10-20 minutes of demonstrating sincerity before moving on to the next phase.

Venting

In this phase the other person begins to believe they can let their guard down and the real information and insights begin to flow.

This is another place in the discussion where you might be tempted to jump in with a solution or some advice. Don't! You will cut off the flow of information and, worse, their thought process.

Many times as sales people we jump in too soon to show how we can help. At this point, the other person is just getting started letting off some steam — simply because someone is actually listening to them! Don't undo what you've already achieved. This part of the discussion is essential in gaining trust so let them go.

When you offer advice or a solution before the other person has completed the venting process, you run into four obstacles:

■ They won't believe you are actually listening. Your body language indicates you aren't fully engaged, which means they don't believe you understand the entire situation (even if you actually do) because you have yet to demonstrate that you have actually heard them.

- The other person is still clarifying, processing, and organizing their own thinking.
- They don't really want to hear the answer. They simply want to talk.
- You are missing cues as to whether or not this prospect is well qualified or not.

Whatever advice or solution you might offer before the venting process is complete could very well be off target because you don't have all the information. Plus, the other person frequently believes that you couldn't possibly have the answer, especially on something they are still struggling with.

To be sure, most of the time you have these types of discussions, you won't have a solution. That doesn't matter. You score points by listening and the customer will ultimately take to *you*, your product, or your solution. The difference in taking this approach is that you don't get yourself into the trap of trying to solve a problem you either don't understand or have the power to fix.

A normal range of expectations is that this phase takes 10-20 minutes, although I have had this phase take as long as 30 minutes.

Truth

You tend to get the real truth and what's really important to the other person at the end of the conversation. There are a couple reasons why this takes time:

- The other person must process whatever issues they have to get to some resolution. Most people need a period of time without interruption to let their minds work.
- We rarely really listen to one another so the privilege of having someone actually listen is, for many, quite therapeutic.

After someone has spoken their mind, most people tend to relax. That can be an advantage for you in understanding the truth about this person's beliefs. While the truth might not be the answer you hoped for, at least you have the truth — or at least this person's vision of it.

If you think about all the meetings you have been to, the best insights always seem to come at the very end.

Wait to Get to Your Product or Solution

How you think your product, services, or company can "help" the customer is **all about you**. But any discussion has to be **about the customer** and what is important to them. So, if you pitch your stuff too soon, you shut down the customer's thinking process and a critical goal of the needs assessment strategy — to get the other person to let you in and get them to a point when they begin to trust you enough to tell you the truth.

Three things happen if you go to product, service, or solution too soon and none of them are good:

- You immediately minimize the vast number of subjects that are open for discussion to only one or two. This is a sure-fire technique to diminish the quantity and quality of information you might get from the customer about something that might help move the sales process forward.
- You might miss a wide range of topics about the business, the organization, their customers, the market, this person's personal goals, their boss, etc. These topics are, in many cases, areas where the customer has expertise, insight, and probably some excellent experience from which you can learn and possibly benefit.
- The conversation is now about something on which they are the novice, not the expert. They are no longer the center of attention — the conversation changes from being about them and who they are to being about you.

By going to product or solution too soon, you risk shutting down the information pipeline. And as they lose interest, they shut down and begin to look for ways to get the conversation over with.

What is always telling to me is how the look on their face(s) and body language changes as they begin to see that you are actually listening. That's when they really start to enjoy the conversation. Imagine that — having fun talking to a sales person!

Saving Time over the Long-Term

By now you might be thinking: *This sounds like a lot of work and risky too. To basically relinquish control of the flow of a sales conversation and let the customer take it where they will - that could be risky!*

You are absolutely right. The first three or four weeks will be spent learning, becoming familiar with the process and how people react. However, what you will notice pretty quickly (in about 10 days) is that you actually spend less time with poorly qualified opportunities. So, over time, this will save you time and energy — in part, because you will have the confidence not to chase poor prospects as often. If you have mastered a way to determine the reality of each opportunity much sooner, you will have time to invest with the most qualified leads.

One of the biggest challenges for any sales person, at any level, is the time spent with prospects and on opportunities that never materialize. Effective use of the needs assessment process will minimize those poorly qualified investments over time as you get better at recognizing the patterns of the most and least qualified.

In fairness, it won't eliminate all bad prospects but most of the professionals we have worked with indicate a 50 percent reduction in over-investing in poorly qualified leads. That's a significant time saver!

What you should expect from customers:

- Inconsistency in some of their answers and attitudes.
    - *Their perspective changes over time.*
    - *They are not sure.*
    - *They have not thought about a particular issue.*
- Most customers will open up right away — you will be amazed at how much they will tell you.
- Some customers will take longer to trust your approach.
- Some, hopefully just a few, will never get there

A key for any sales person it to identify which each group the prospect is in, at that point deciding what to do next is much simpler. This takes practice but will become much easier over time.

Knowing When There Is an Opportunity

I'm often asked, *So, how many of these meetings do I need to have to know if I should proceed or not?* Generally, you can usually tell in one or two meetings. If you get to the third meeting and you don't feel good about the progress that you are making, then your amygdala is probably working just fine.

Alternatively, you can ask yourself these questions, preceded with a *How close am I to learning...*

- *...if there is a real opportunity or am I being unrealistic?*
- *...if there is real pain or interest on the part of the customer?*
- *...if I understand enough about their decision process to proceed?*
- *...if I have a strong solution to solve their issue?*
- *...about how difficult the financial, distribution/logistics pieces are?*

Finally, is the opportunity worthy of your investment in time, money, and mental energy now or not? My answer is always the same — based on what you have seen and learned so far, what does your amygdala tell you?

The next chapter has examples of needs assessment interviews so you might want to take a break before reading any further. It will be interesting to compare your experiences to what we learned with clients.

Chapter 6

Conducting the Discussion: Needs Assessment Examples

In this chapter, we will examine a group of sales scenarios where the needs assessment interviews were conducted with client sales teams and customers or prospective customers. I conducted most of the interviews as they took place while in the modeling behavior part of training my clients. As each sales person progressed during our training, they gradually learned the process and adapted their own, unique style of conducting these conversations.

In most cases these were very basic and simple calls. Most selling situations we find ourselves in every day are essentially very basic, although they require hard and, often, tedious work. Success in learning new skills is, in many ways, a function of our own ability and willingness to do the basics like the grunt work and other unexciting stuff like due diligence on the customer and his or her organization.

You will find that we were often required to venture outside a typical sales person's comfort zone. This was validated and continues to be validated by our ongoing interactions with our colleagues and customers. We've found that if we act only within our own comfort zones, we almost never get the best insights or sales results. The key in this entire process is to expand your comfort zone, which this process will help you do over time and at your own pace.

Fully realizing this point seems redundant and may even sound obvious. Yet so many clients I talk to tell me that, to them, sales people are not often willing or able to work within the customer's comfort zone. They only seem to be comfortable in their own comfort zone which generally does not include listening or truly engaging with their customers using the needs assessment process — listening to get to sincerity, venting, and truth.

The fundamental principles and learning opportunities in each of these examples (including one when the process didn't work out as we had hoped) has much more to do with behavioral science principles and how those apply to every sales situation — in any industry. Each situation and customer will vary but the fundamental principles of human communication do not. As mentioned at the beginning of this book, this approach will absolutely improve your success but is not perfect. No process is perfect.

Four Scenarios

Most needs assessment interviews (sales calls) generally occur within one of four sets of circumstances. These are the four scenarios where the needs assessment skills can really make a difference:

- **Benign Complacency:** We have a current customer and think we are in good shape with them but have not really validated that assumption.
- **Trouble:** We know we are in jeopardy and it is probably pretty bad.
- **Missing or Sunken Proposal:** A business proposal is stalled because there is a new management structure, a new decision-making process, or both. It is almost as if it vanished and no one seems willing to acknowledge that it ever existed.
- **Blank Piece of Paper:** We have no relationship or not much of a relationship, not enough information, or we are starting over even if we have known the prospect for some time.

In these examples, I will talk about what happened, how the customers and clients reacted, what we learned, and suggestions for some ways you might conduct these types of conversations in your own world. You will immediately notice that the lines between these scenarios are very grey. The circumstances and details in each of the examples can and will run together. One thing is certain — you are missing some key element(s) of the story. Sometimes you don't learn what it is until it's too late.

However, in each case we were able to find out the real issues, how decisions were made, and determine our chances of success within the following 30-90 days. Let me be clear. We did not get the answer we were hoping for every time. However, we did get to the truth. As you will see, we also learned enough to be very confident about what or what not to do next.

Each scenario involves different people and circumstances. Yet as we went through this series of sales calls, some very similar patterns — patterns that probably apply to your professional world — emerged in each of these unique situations. We noticed these specific patterns:

- The more we used the Silent Selling approach, the more insight we gained to tell us exactly what to do next and with much greater confidence. At times, we couldn't save the business so we knew not to over invest in attempting the improbable. Each time, the right next steps became very clear.
- We validated the sincerity, venting, and truth patterns every time.

Most importantly for me (and you, if you are a manager) is that the client recognized the efficacy of the system and wanted to learn how to get better at doing it now that they had seen it work.

Scenario 1: Benign Complacency

We think the customer is happy but we're not absolutely sure.

This is a classic situation for most sales people. We think things are going well even though we have very little empirical data to support that belief. We might have checked to see if they are actually still purchasing from us but typically not much beyond that. No one has called with problems or to complain and all the signs and information we have at our disposal indicate nothing has changed.

Oftentimes, we find out that things aren't going as well as we had thought or hoped only when the boss comes to work with us or we receive some initiative from marketing or management to further penetrate our existing customers.

Example 1:
Luxury Hotel, Half Moon Bay, CA

We made this call with a client sales person (let's call her Mary) on an existing customer, a luxury hotel in Half Moon Bay, California. The goal was to expand distribution or sell more into an existing account. (This scenario would also be applicable if the goal was to extend the contract with an existing customer, provided you had not confirmed if they were happy or not with your overall performance.)

Mary assured me the customer (let's call him Jonathan) was happy with her company and service yet she had not really defined or validated what "happy" meant to them. Yet she wanted to sell them something else — something on which her credibility had not yet been established. It was not a customer need that had been identified or defined — she thinks it's there because, well, they should buy it.

At this point, as the outside consultant, I am not ready to rain on her parade. My thinking was to let her see the call go off track so she would then see the truth of the situation.

The meeting got off to a very slow start as Mary went right to her product and what *she wanted to happen — not listening or engaging her client in the needs assessment steps.* That lasted for about 10 very painful minutes, judging by the look on the customer's face and his body language (he looked at his watch at least twice). Finally, sensing that this wasn't going well, and with my assignment for the day to help Mary in exactly this type of situation, I jumped in with a series of questions demonstrating sincerity and showing I was listening:

■ *So, Jonathan, as Mary and I were walking around the property before our scheduled meeting, we noticed the breakfast buffet. How does all that work?*

During his explanation, he made a comment about the General Manager's preference for something. That was a clue. He was giving a hint as to the identity of the real decision maker.

■ *Interesting, how would you describe his approach on that?*

He talked for several more minutes, letting on — indirectly at first — that his boss, the hotel General Manager, was very involved in most of the food and beverage decisions and strategy.

- Then I asked, *One of the things we were wondering about is how the organization (hotel) decides to make a menu change or a vendor change. How does that work?*
- I paused here and then continued with, *Since we are outsiders, could you share with us how that has worked in the past and how all the pieces of the process work? Such as, who does what and how they decide which vendors to work with? Frankly, so far we have been guessing. Your view would really help us.*

He told us, in no uncertain terms, that **he did not have the power or authority** that he once had. He also shared with us how frustrating that was for him personally.

I had coached Mary to just sit there and listen, nod her head, and limit her responses to, *Really, how so?* or to simply repeat whatever he said followed by, *I think I have an idea what you are getting at. Could you give me more detail?* As a result, he kept talking (venting) for at least another 20-25 minutes.

This gave us a clear direction on what to focus. We gained his endorsement for us to reach out to the General Manager and to help him sell up in the organization. This, after he had been very clear in sharing with us that the General Manager was "a tough person to convince."

This would certainly explain why her previous proposals did almost nothing to get additional business with this client. He couldn't sell up, he didn't have the authority he once did, or his boss didn't have the confidence in him to make any real or important decisions.

Using Sincerity, Venting, and Truth

By asking the question very indirectly (after he had been talking for about 15 of the last 20 minutes) and waiting until he hinted that the General Manager influenced these decisions and discussing how that had impacted him personally, I had let him relax and encouraged him to continue talking about what was important to him. We were beginning to see the sincerity, venting, and truth patterns emerge. Then we got the gold. *He can't actually make many decisions without involving the General Manager.* So, expecting this person, or someone at his level, to make the call was something that would have been a mistake for both Mary and me.

If we had stayed focused on what was important to us, such as selling something else, the results would have been much different. We would have never engaged Jonathan in a way that got him to think about the business and volunteer that he really couldn't make the decision about adding another menu item without the General Manager's approval. The meeting would have been over in 15 minutes.

What we learned as we continued to call on some of the other hotel accounts in Northern California was that most Directors of Food and Beverage can't make important decisions about their restaurants, suppliers, and menus without getting buy-in from the General Manager. The more General Managers we talked to, the more this was validated.

Common Mistakes

Like most sales people, Mary is charming, driven, smart, organized, and very successful. But even she didn't see the trend around the loss of decision-making autonomy of hotel Food and Beverage Directors in her own market — and she had been selling there for at least three years. At the same time, she had not spent enough time or energy gathering information and understanding how these organizations work and make decisions. It wasn't something her manager or her organization had ever thought was important enough to be a top priority.

This is a classic case of working against the wrong objective based on flawed assumptions. Mary's manager had never coached her or encouraged her to use all of her intellectual horsepower to gather the necessary information. His mantra had always been, *Tell them how good we are*. Once she gave herself permission to not know everything and use her intellect, it didn't take long for Mary to figure this out on her own.

Later in the interview, we asked Jonathan what operations he was most proud of and what he would do with the facilities if the decisions were his own. He said, *Let me show you*, and proceeded to show us around the property. He spent about another hour with us — we had originally been scheduled for 30 minutes.

Asking a customer about their vision for their business or their specific area is a great way to gain valuable insight about what matters to them. It is also a great way to find out who calls the shots, this person's limits and range of influence, and how decisions are really made in the organization.

If they will tell you what they like and what frustrates them about their company or organization, it gives you additional insight into how progressive the customer's organization truly is or is not. And that has a direct relationship to your upside revenue potential within that organization. This technique works about 75 percent of the time. If they are not capable or don't have a vision, that will become evident as well.

Following this discussion, Jonathan gave Mary three new, solid opportunities that were much greater in sales, revenue, and margins than what she had focused on originally.

Four things happened during the call:

- We took the sales pressure off — that was the first step. Given the permission to be candid about that, most customers will tell you that they hate sales pressure but feel it way too often.
- We changed the conversation from what we cared about to what he cared about.
- We actually listened. Then we responded to what we were hearing from him.
- He began to figure out how we could help him because we had helped him clarify his thoughts.

Later in the day, we ran into the General Manager of a large downtown San Francisco Hotel. I asked him one question:

One of the things we are trying to get smarter about is how the Food and Beverage Directors work with their General Managers in making decisions about the menu, the products they use, and all of that. Could you help us understand how that works from your industry perspective?

He proceeded to tell us quite a bit, including the real decision-making powers of Food and Beverage Managers. Their powers center around staffing, setting schedules, and making sure the logistics pieces work properly. When it comes to changing the menu or vendors, he was very clear — General Managers almost always have the final say.

He also added that any Food and Beverage Manager with enough political skill to survive in a successful hotel knows very well that they must keep the General Manager in the loop. We also learned that most General Managers are reluctant to relinquish their authority or power to the Food and Beverage Manager.

Having this General Manager tell these things to Mary was very effective in getting her to look at the larger picture. His comments, combined with our experience earlier in the day, started a process of new learning.

Points to Consider and Remember

Before you try to sell another product to an existing customer, step back and get an update on what is going on in the organization, including current priorities. Again, the goal in this discussion is to get them to open up and give you their perspective and, ultimately, their view of what is going on inside their organization — then you can figure what you can sell them and how difficult that might be. Otherwise, you are working toward a very poorly defined opportunity with a very low chance of success.

The secret trick is that you actually have to be listening very carefully and maintaining eye contact. That means you can't be thinking about or distracted by anything else (this includes leaving your cell phone in the car so there is no chance it will distract you or your customer). If you are completely engaged two things will happen — your body language will show it (which is 80 percent of all communication) and you will really get the information in context and know how to proceed.

Scenario 2: Trouble

We know we are in jeopardy and it is probably pretty bad.

When you are in a hole and want to get out of it, the first thing you need to do is quit digging.

In this scenario, we know the customer is unhappy and the account is in jeopardy. When you know it's bad, I recommend going right to that. I always ask, *Is this over? Have you decided you are not going to work with us going forward?*

Many people are very uncomfortable with this approach. Some view it as too risky, bold, or even disrespectful. My rationale is simple. Don't run the risk of insulting them by trying to mask the truth. Get right to the point and then let them vent. Yet if you are not comfortable with that approach, then don't use it — you can take a softer approach. The point is they *will* vent. You just might not be in the room when they do. The question is: *Do you want to know what the issues are or not?*

To make this approach effective, you must be willing to use the "curiously humble" mind-set. If you, your company, or your staff dropped the ball, then fess up. The worst thing you can do is ***not*** take responsibility.

Example 1:
Family-Owned Dining Chain, Chicago, IL

In this case, a long-time customer simply had not been managed properly nor paid the proper amount of attention. To be sure, the customer was having issues of their own but our client still had to own the fact that they had taken this customer for granted. And the customer knew it.

If the other person is really angry or frustrated, you have to be prepared to, and capable of, letting them vent — even if the problem is not directly your fault. You represent the company. You cash the regular paychecks and use the benefits. So yes, like it or not, this is part of your job as a professional.

If you are so frustrated with your company and the company's service failures and policies that you can't (in good faith) defend your company and fight for the account, it's time to find another job.

I get some pushback on this approach, so let me explain why I believe in it (other than the fact I have seen it work countless times). You have undoubtedly heard that you can minimize customer service issues or service failures by simply admitting fault and then working to get the situation resolved. We have all seen businesses that are really good at this (Southwest Airlines and Starbucks come to mind) and those that are not (cable companies and most airlines).

Most of the problems come from a customer's feeling that they are being disrespected or the sales person lacks sincerity. As such, you don't want to start out the conversation patronizing the other person as though there is something they don't understand. You must be willing to acknowledge that their perspective matters. Don't exacerbate the tension by trivializing their challenges or issues. It's insulting and a very bad way to resolve an issue or keep an account. You can immediately alleviate much of the tension by just letting them vent.

To start, consider using these statements, as appropriate:

- *I dropped the ball. We dropped the ball. No question.*
- *That's fair. I didn't see it that way before.*
- *These are not our standards and I am personally embarrassed.*
- *It feels to me that I didn't meet your expectations and that you are disappointed.*
- *What can be done to resolve the matter?*
- *In your view, is this beyond repair? Is this over?*

This does not, however, mean being obsequious or apologizing for something that is not your responsibility. It is simply an adult-to-adult discussion. Think about the last time you switched vendors, changed dry cleaners, or made some other change with who you do business with personally or professionally. By the time you considered taking action, you had probably been thinking about it for some time already. You may have been frustrated for weeks but one issue, at the right time, set you off.

There is a tremendous difference between saying, *I am sorry and frankly embarrassed that we could not or did not meet your expectations. That's not right,* and an insincere, *Sorry about that. We are sorry for your inconvenience.* That last response is completely canned and phony and the customer senses it — we have all gotten that type of reaction from a credit card company, cable company, or airline. The former acknowledges the problem and the person whom the problem affected and the latter does not.

I recently learned of an approach that really impressed me and is used by a number of full-service chain restaurant companies — the LAST protocol. It consists of four steps to be completed in this order: Listen, Apologize, Solve, and Thank. You'll notice that the first step is to listen.

Recovery Guidelines:

- Make the conversation adult-to-adult. You cannot get defensive or make the conversation about you. For example, don't use any of the techniques — if you can call them that — that some of the major airlines and credit card companies employ: *It's not my fault...I didn't know...I don't make the rules...That's just our policy... It's for your protection.* Those are child-to-adult discussions — attempts to extricate oneself from any responsibility and make you go away. The other person senses and feels the phoniness or duplicity.

- Go into the needs assessment mind-set using your own style. Here's one way:
  - *It is clear to me that we have really screwed up here and probably should have known about this sooner. So shame on us.*
  - *It sounds like we didn't meet your expectations or our own frankly. And that is not only unfortunate; it is embarrassing to me personally and professionally.*
  - *Having said that, may I ask you some questions about how long this has been an issue and about some of the other things that I don't see or understand?*
  - *Can you start from the beginning and tell me what you think I need to know to understand your perspective?*

- Next, use silence. Nod your head, take notes (or not), and let them vent. This will tell you how bad it really is (or isn't).

If the customer will not have this discussion with you or you can't fix the issues in a timely manner, you are probably on the way to losing the business. In the case of the Chicago-based family dining chain, our client did lose the business. Frankly, they deserved to lose it. This example is included because, as realists, you and I both know these situations are out there and you need to learn to handle them like a professional.

The one positive that did come out of this situation was that our client discovered some simple challenges and issues they were able to resolve that helped in preventing some additional losses of business. Losing the restaurant chain was not the answer they were hoping for but at least they got the truth and gained some valuable insight that helped them move forward with other accounts.

Points to Consider and Remember

Among the challenges in this scenario is that you come into the process when the customer is more than half way to quitting. They have already been thinking about the issues and have become frustrated by a lack of response or some other issue. So yes, you get hit like a ton of bricks.

What this means to you is that they are much further down the path of being impacted by whatever the issues are and, more than likely, are getting some significant internal, political pressure that can be a much larger problem than you realize. You don't ever want to be the source of political problems for your customer — that is a sure way to lose their support and business.

You don't ever want to be the source of political problems for your customer — that is a sure way to lose their support and the business.

Scenario 3: The Missing or Sunken Proposal

A business proposal is stalled because there is a new management structure, a new decision-making process, or both. It is almost as if it vanished and no one seems willing to acknowledge that it ever existed.

Example 1:
Beach Front Hotel, Daytona Beach, FL

In this case, we were calling on a hotel in Florida during their peak season. The sales person (let's call him Robert) had made a new proposal, about 60 days prior to our visit, to gain additional business. He had received very little in the way of a response — even after completing the needs assessment process and due diligence before making the proposal. His contacts had been accessible but vague. Robert's amygdala was on high alert, as it should have been.

Robert had good relationships with both the Food and Beverage Director and the General Manager. What we found was that the company had been purchased by a new owner — a group that owns multiple hotel brands — and both his contacts had simply lost their decision-making power on any number of issues.

As you read through this example, you will see many of the same patterns as in the first scenario — internal decision-making processes and pressures were not what we thought they were. But we had to let the customer tell us that — sensitive or new information has much more credibility if the other person tells you first. This is another reminder to not make assumptions, even if you already know the answer.

Robert, to his credit, did not simply launch into a sales pitch. He worked with the needs assessment process to find out what was really going on with this customer. In turn, the customer read the sincerity on Robert's part and was very candid about the company's reorganization. So at the end of the meeting, Robert had a much better grasp on what approach would work best and a strong feeling about how much to invest with this customer.

During the meeting, we went into the same type of questions as the previous examples, although this time it was much easier for me, as the consultant, because Robert had done a good job of asking questions prior to the meeting and knew the hotel had been for sale. So he began on the right foot by starting with, *You mentioned on the phone that there had been some changes. What's going on since we last talked?*

Spending time and gathering information by asking about changes can shed light on some real challenges. This is especially true if the changes are a surprise to the current team running the business or the new owners are strictly financial buyers who are new to the industry. Those new to an industry tend to overestimate the subtle complexities and their understanding of the business. A vast majority of them also start off by undervaluing the views, practices, and perspectives of those who have been in the industry or the organization for some time. If you have ever been in this situation, then you know exactly how that feels. It can be very difficult since established business practices, cultures, and expectations no longer matter as much, if at all.

We first learned that the Food and Beverage Manager was close to taking another position with a competitor. So Robert began to connect with the General Manager to learn more about how he could help with that new situation. The General Manager stayed with the hotel and, as a result of the Food and Beverage Manager leaving, needed help with new revenue opportunities.

One idea to come out of it was a coffee bar concept — which my client was more than happy to help him with. Although it took Robert about 60 days to earn the trust of the General Manager, the result was that he was no longer just a sales person. He had come to be seen more as a trusted business partner. Robert found new opportunities all because he took the time to get to know the business and the people by following the needs assessment process.

What we found conducting this interview was that they needed a new overall strategy for their entire operation. Ultimately, as a result of the reorganization, Robert lost some business (which turned out to be the lower margin segment of the business), but gained some incremental business in another area of the hotel — the new coffee bar, which had much higher profit margins and fewer headaches than the regular coffee business.

Points to Consider and Remember

You simply must get to what is important to the customer. Because there are new owners, new priorities, and new organizational dynamics, you need to understand enough about their business and priorities to ask compelling enough questions to stimulate a meaningful discussion.

The most difficult part of this type of scenario is interpreting what is going on with the professionals that you have been working with in the past — especially senior operations managers. As an outsider, you must become even more diligent about understanding the structural and cultural changes in play. When a financial buyer comes into a new organization, those who have actually run the business and been your customers face these challenges:

- New owners may or may not have real operating competencies.
- New loyalties or no loyalties at all.
- The evaluation criteria are changing and no one is truly sure of the new criteria. This can lead to mass confusion about job responsibilities.

All of these factors can adversely affect, even end, a sales person's relationship with a client.

Today there is quite a bit of merger and acquisition activity in any number of industries and, given the volatility in the economy and financial markets, these patterns are likely to continue. These "financial buyers" usually fall into one of three groups:

- Those who don't care about the craft of the business. They want to take some costs out of the business so that over time it can be positioned for another sale. This group may or may not be good to work with.
- Those who want to upgrade to generate more revenue and keep current customers. This group can be really good to work with.
- Those who either won't share their new business goals, are not sure what they are, or want the status quo. This group is a wild card.

Let's take a look at trends and patterns of consolidation in the hotel business occurring over the past 18 months as an example:

- **Industry Consolidation:** Financially driven investment business models. The reality of this dynamic will impact your career as a sales person in a number of ways.
  - o Those professionals who have actually run these businesses, who have been educated and trained on the business, the craft of serving their customers, and the industry organizational culture often lose power when new owners come in. Or worse, they become discouraged, frustrated, and ineffective.
  - o When the ownership structure changes, a new owner is often focused on maximizing ROI and minimizing expenditures. Many of these buyers either undervalue or don't care about the skills, tools, and practices of the trade. In most cases, the goal is to resell the business at a profit 3-7 years after the purchase.

To you, this means that your needs assessment skills are even more important than ever. You need to find out who the new buying influences are and what the new priorities are and whether they are worth an investment of your time and resources.

- **Buying Influences:** We often get very different insight from each of the buying influences at a company. Each of them typically has their own perspective on the company's priorities and needs. One of the challenges during a merger or acquisition is that no one really knows much about the new owners who likely have their own agenda and may or may not be willing to share with the existing team. (You have probably seen this before in your industry.)

One idea to get some additional insight is to get permission from your contact to ask them about their perspective on the ownership change or the new boss and see how he or she reacts.

To start these discussions, I always suggest using questions in this situation such as:

- *How do you see the new structure impacting your role?*
- *How would you describe the new person's style? What seem to be the priorities?*
- *How do they view the role of your function in the overall success of the business?*
- *As an outsider, what are some the challenges that you are facing that I might not see?*

The key is to get each person involved in the three phases of the needs assessment process and help them work through the organizational shift.

Example 2:
Hotel, San Francisco, CA

You have certainly been through this. You prepare a proposal for what you think is a well-qualified opportunity. Then it all goes off track and seems as though the proposal simply vanished.

This one had many similarities to the previous example — the sales person (let's call her Janet) had known and worked with these folks for about five years. She had made a proposal to the Director of Food and Beverage to upgrade and add some additional products, which her primary contact had really liked. Then it stalled. She shared with me that, *It was like we had never talked about it all of a sudden and we had talked about it a lot!*

What we found out as the meeting progressed was that her contact had (much to Janet's surprise), in fact, given her proposal to his boss for his final OK — four weeks earlier. So far there was no response. And Janet's contact person didn't want to create any unnecessary tension with his boss by forcing the issue. Who can blame him for that?

Even with good qualifying questions with decision makers in the needs assessment process, we have all seen things get murky when it comes to decision time. The politics typically play out behind closed doors.

The other factor in play is that many customers will ask you for a proposal just to get you out of their office. Later, they can always claim that some outside, higher force changed direction without their knowledge or asking for their input.

There are three approaches to use here. Two are fairly common and ineffective — the do-nothing approach or using a range of aggressiveness in follow up. The least utilized, and to some the most risky, is the "I guess since we haven't heard from you, you went in another direction" approach. This is the one I recommend and here's how it works.

The next time you haven't heard back from a prospect in the agreed time frame, use this version of an old insurance sales person's technique called the negative reverse. It is an older one but it works about 50-60 percent of the time. While that might not sound like much, it beats the other two alternatives and at least gets you an answer. Try leaving a voicemail message (as they have likely stopped taking your calls at this point) or having a discussion along these lines:

- *We haven't heard back from you and we certainly don't want to be a nuisance but we just didn't want to drop the ball on our end.*
- *Usually when we don't hear back from a client by now, it means they have either gone in another direction, selected another vendor, or the project isn't a priority today. And that is OK. We would just like to confirm where things are so we don't tie people up on our end or learn what to do better next time.*
- *So at this point, should we assume that this project is not going to happen? If we get some type of confirmation from you that this is no longer a realistic possibility, we will just close the file on this one.*

Do not contact your customer with any unsolicited offer for additional clarification or information. The worst message you can leave is one that sounds desperate, such as, *I was just calling to see if you needed anything or had any questions about the proposal.* You look foolish doing this.

71

Sadly, this is an admission of frustration and uncertainty. They know perfectly well that if they need more information or clarification on a point, they can contact you. The only exception is if there is some truly compelling reason to introduce new information or remind them of a pending deadline — usually one imposed on your side.

Points to Consider and Remember

You must be honest with yourself here. You want to know what is going on and why they haven't been in communication. The fact is, in most cases, they simply don't need you right now. If their job was to get the information or the RFP completed, then their fiduciary responsibility has been completed. Even when you do everything right, that is going to happen — hopefully with less frequency when you begin to use these principles.

Having made this point, you are perfectly within professional protocol to ask for feedback or how things are going internally. Questions such as:

- *I'm just very curious as to what initial feedback you might have for us?*
- *How are we doing on the original time line for feedback and updates or next steps?* (Of course, they almost never are on the original time line. At some point someone has to make a decision. This involves risk and usually procrastination.)
- *We were interested to know how on or off target we were on the key points.*
- *As you might imagine, there is quite a bit of interest at our place on how things are going on your end — any advice or information as to what I might share with my team?*

We have all been through this many times. It always gets interesting when the customer organization has to actually make a decision and, up until now, really hasn't had to do too much other than go to meetings and ask for proposals. Now the work and the political machinations go into full swing inside their organization.

What's important to remember about the sunken or missing proposal is that while many factors might contribute to it, only a proper needs assessment discussion will reveal the true nature of the stalled opportunity. You must get to the root of the confusion by allowing those involved to feel comfortable sharing new information. That starts with asking the right questions, then listening.

Scenario 4: Blank Piece of Paper

We have no relationship or not much of one, not enough information, or are starting over even if we have known the prospect for some time.

This scenario can come about in a couple of different ways. It could be a cold call (no relationship at all) or the result of incomplete or flawed initial interviews where there was not enough information gathered and it's best to simply start over.

I get questions about how to go about this frequently, especially from senior level sales people who have been calling on some of the same customers for years. One question I seem to hear most is, *I have been calling on them for so long. How do I go in there now and ask a bunch of questions that I probably should have been asking before or should already have the answers to?*

First things first. Give yourself permission to not be perfect! Then take the "blank piece of paper" approach — if you could start with a blank piece of paper, how would you structure the business relationship? What would it look like? What really matters to the customer? How would you approach helping them achieve what is important to them?

In today's business world, everyone is dealing with new issues, fewer resources, and new pressures. Many find it therapeutic to have a discussion about their world if the other person is really listening and engaged, especially someone they have known for a while. This is particularly true if they respect or trust the other person.

In restarting a dialogue or changing the nature of a relationship or previous patterns, consider some of these guidelines:

- Acknowledge that the situation has changed.
- Determine what you want to accomplish and share that with the other person.
- Ask for permission to ask questions.
- Ask for help in understanding.
- Show genuine curiosity and humility.
- Use silence.

Your attitude and body language really matters here. This is a feeling-out process for the customer and they will want to be confident in your sincerity.

Many tenured sales people have confided in me that they are more than a little embarrassed they have gone so long and not had this conversation with their customer. That is OK. Simply tell the customer (or your spouse, close friend, or loved one) that you have been thinking about this and it occurred to you that you don't have all the insight you think is important to the relationship.

The goal is to take the pressure off and keep the conversation adult-to-adult so that you get the insights and information you need. Here are some ways to start that conversation. These next questions are just guidelines. Wordsmith them so they sound like you.

- *We have known each other for some time and have accomplished a lot. What I would like to work on today may be considered a bit unique. In thinking about your business and our relationship, it feels to me like there are some things about your business I need to better understand. So, if it's alright with you, what I would like to do today is gather information and get your insight on…*
- *I am not here to sell anything today. I know that in the past I would typically come in and show you products but what I would like to do today is a little different.*
- *With what I learn today, I'd like to do some additional thinking about how or if we can help and then schedule a follow-up visit where we could discuss some ideas that are designed specifically to help you with what is important to you. As part of that, let's agree that if neither one of us sees that we have any common interests today, then we can revisit the subject at a later time or not, if that works better for you.*
    - *What are the factors that have impacted you the most recently?*
    - *There is a lot going on out there today, so what's changed in your world, with your business, with your organization, customers, etc.*
- *What do I need to know to help you out?*
- *What are the one or two pieces of information or insight that I probably don't have that would help me better understand…?* (Fill in the blank or just stop there. About 80% of the time the other person will give you some good insight.)
- *We have worked together before and a lot has evolved in the business. What are the two or three things that strike you as the most significant?*
- *How have those issues impacted you?*
- *I have been studying some of the industry trends and it has occurred to me some things have changed in your business. Would you be willing to help me get smarter about your business?*

- *What advice would you give me about how to get smarter about what is happening in your world? Maybe some of the important insight that I might not see?*
- *Since I don't work here, I am sure there are some fundamental things that I just don't see. What are the two or three that you think would help me better understand the conditions you are working under?*
- *Given the challenges in the industry today, what are some of things your best vendors are doing the makes them stand out in your mind?*

Most of the time, these types of questions will totally disarm the other person, if you come across as sincere. The key here is that you have to actually mean it and then "walk the talk" by getting in and staying in the needs assessment mind-set and behaviors.

Example 1: Starting Over
Chain Restaurant Company, based in Dallas, TX

A client of mine (we'll call him Pete) was trying to understand how an organization made vendor decisions. He had relationships with people within the organization and had made proposals in the past but nothing had ever turned into business. (Sound familiar?)

Pete finally got comfortable with the fact that despite his long tenure in knowing this company, he simply didn't know how these folks made decisions. That was his first step and a big one for him.

To illustrate the point, I simply asked him to describe to me his history and experience with this account. While he was doing that I wrote the major points and some details on a white board. When he was done, we reviewed and then I said to him, *Erase it from your mind*, as I erased the white board so we could start over with a blank, fresh sheet of paper.

Once he got over not knowing everything, we were able to develop an approach that got him closer to the real decision process.

There is a tremendous amount of tension and interest around this subject today. Massive amounts of time, money, and energy have been spent on trying to better understand how customers make business decisions. There are books and business school studies dedicated to the subject.

This is also a touchy subject for many customer organizations for at least one of four reasons:

- How they make business decisions as an organization is rarely something that a company wants to share with vendors. Many see this process as confidential, something that is an internal matter.
- The last thing senior management wants is their team members sharing confidential insights with vendors. They want them working on *their business with their customers.*
- Many times, the person(s) you are working with are only part of the decision process, if at all. The challenge can come in two ways — either they are not comfortable sharing their role with you or they have an inaccurate view of their role in the decision process.
- There may not be a clearly defined process for making decisions.

I never directly ask, and advise you not to either, *Who makes the decisions?* or *Are you the decision maker?* There are two reasons for this. First, that direct approach can be threatening and, as such, an ineffective technique for getting the insight you need. Second, you run the risk of getting a very short answer without much insight, which doesn't help you nearly as much as a broader, deeper answer with context and insights.

There are much better ways to get the answer to that question by using a softer, more open-ended approach. These are questions clients have used and, in this case, Pete used with at least three of his contacts inside the organization — a protocol that has become part of our process at Bellwether Food Group and used by other clients. As part of the first discussion, you can start down the path with one of these questions:

- *Today, if it's OK with you, I wanted to get your perspective on some things that maybe we haven't talked about before and maybe even ask you for some advice. Would that be OK?*
- *Could you help me understand a little more about your organization and how things work here?* (This is the permission question. Make sure they answer that specific question, affirmatively. If they won't answer or stall, ask them if the question is appropriate or fair in their view. If they won't have the discussion with you, then you have your answer!)
- *When you think about one of the last times you have changed or made a major shift with vendors or added something new to the company, could you*

share with me your view of how all that worked? Who was involved? (Use silence here!)

At this point in the discussion, you need to do three things:

- Fight the urge to jump in and offer solutions or comment on what you are hearing. You might throw them off course and disrupt the sincerity, venting, and truth dynamic.
- Ask for clarification using phrases such as:
  - *Really?*
  - *How so?*
  - *How well did that work?*
- After you have heard three points, summarize by saying, *So can we take a minute here, just so I can make sure I am following you and getting it right?* Then, tell them what you have heard. If it is going well, they will either interrupt or add something — that's good!

My preference is to use the phrase, *So, let me make sure I have this right.* or *May I summarize what I have heard so far, just to make sure I have it right in my mind?*

You can continue with some follow-up questions, such as:

- *As an outsider to the organization, what insight would you share with me about what I would not see or know about how things work here?*
- *Going forward, what advice would you give me?*
  (Again, fight the urge to jump in. Be sure to use silence and summarize after every second or third point made by the customer.)
- *Anything else?* Followed by, you guessed it, silence.

You have basically asked the same question now three times, possibly even four times. Over the course of thousands of sales calls, my personal experience is that it typically takes about this long to find out three important facts:

- Whether or not this person really knows how decisions are made within the organization.
- How much this person's professional input matters to the final decision.

- How they view the structure of the organization and the current decision processes his or her organization utilizes and whether or not this person is in agreement with them or not.

This part of the conversation typically takes 10-30 minutes. Interestingly, you usually don't need to ask all the questions to get the insight and information you need. Yet, it is essential to cover all these bases in one way or another. In this case, Pete gathered much more insight than ever before. He was really pleased with what he had learned.

The inevitable question comes at this point from most of my clients, *So, what do you do if they won't tell you anything or simply don't know the answers?* As we touched on previously, this is not the answer you were looking for, the non-answer. Yet, the fact that they don't know or can't or won't tell you the answers speaks volumes about where they fit in the overall process.

If they don't know the decision process or aren't comfortable sharing it with you, then generally speaking, their votes don't count for much in the decision process.

Points to Consider and Remember

The key here is how you ask the questions. They must be wide and open-ended. You cannot ask truly direct questions about the decision process and expect to get the truth. If you ask direct or closed questions, you will get direct answers — which are guaranteed to be brief and may or may not be truly accurate. What you want to get from this discussion are four things:

- How do they really make decisions? Does this person know all the factors?
- Who has the power and who doesn't?
- What role does this person play?
- What are some of the other priorities for the customer?

Anyone who has been in sales for longer than a few months learns quickly that most customer organizations get very confusing and challenging when roles get reversed and the time comes for the customer to make a decision — a form of risk-taking and investment.

So far, the sales person has been making the investments, taking the risks, and doing the work. Now the time has come for the customer to decide. This is when you see the internal political machinations really come into play.

In this case, Pete realized that it was a 6-18 month sales process for new items and that his best bet was to get connected with one of the marketing initiatives coming up in the next 12 months, rather than playing the RFP game against incumbent suppliers. He had learned from one of his interviews that this company rarely changed vendors on existing products unless there was some major issue. But, as a publicly traded company, they felt the need to through the RFP process every time.

Of course, this does not mean that the RFP process is always just an exercise — but it was at this organization. And in Pete's case, he learned a very valuable fact by conducting needs assessment interviews. Otherwise, this could have ended up being a costly and time-consuming, fruitless account.

Example 2: No Relationship
Fresno Sherriff Department, Fresno, CA

Our visit to the Fresno Sherriff Department was incredibly fun. We talked our way into jail!

While working with a client in the coffee business, a sales person in central California we'll call Joe, it occurred to us that we should ask a fundamental question — who drinks a lot of coffee? The first people that came to my mind were police officers. I will bet the police department doesn't get many sales people cold calling without an appointment. It turns out they don't. But this one worked out quite well.

A police station has some interesting characteristics as it relates to food and beverage:

- The environment is intense and can be stressful.
- Much of the staff is stuck inside the building with limited breaks from the pressure of the job.
- They need to be alert.

You might be thinking that this level of sales call is beneath your place in the business world and that's certainly fair. At the same time, this was a great learning experience for getting through a gatekeeper. It was, of course, an armed gatekeeper no less!

Often the first thing you hear when walking into a business is, *What firm are you with?* or *How are you?* or *Do you have an appointment?* So, how do you get around that? Be curious, humble, and on message. Here's what we did, without an appointment:

Gatekeeper/Police Sergeant: *Can I help you? Do you have an appointment here?*

First, let us apologize for stopping by without an appointment. We have been planning to learn more about your operation here, had an unexpected cancellation of an appointment today, and wondered if you could direct us to the person who is responsible for buying and providing the coffee to the staff here? We certainly realize that this may not be a good time but since we were across the street, it made sense to at least give it a try.

Gatekeeper/Police Sergeant: *What company are you with and what is your name?*

My name is Mac and I am working with Joe today from [Coffee Company]. What's your name, officer?

Gatekeeper/Police Sergeant: *I am Officer Jones. You want to speak with Lt. Ramirez. Let me see if he is available.*

We waited about 10-15 minutes and then Lt. Ramirez appeared and escorted us back to the cafeteria, where it was lunchtime. Lt. Ramirez turned out to be a true gentleman, spending about 30 minutes with us telling us all about the who, where, what, when, and how of the foodservice operations throughout the county.

Of course, we encouraged him to talk by starting with this:

- *Thank you for seeing us without an appointment. We have been talking about reaching out to the sheriff's department and happened to be in the neighborhood, so we thought we would take a chance.*
- *We're sure you prefer to work with appointments, as we do, but we are just very curious about how all of this works?*
- *So, as outsiders what do we need to understand about how the county buys food and coffee for all the employees?*

Lt. Ramirez spoke for about 20-25 minutes straight, almost without stopping. How did we get him to do that?

First, in fairness, this involved a certain amount of luck — him actually being there, our getting in, and that he turned out to be a nice guy and a gentleman to boot.

At the same time, the Silent Selling principles really worked here. Specifically, we were humble and curious. We were also in the mind-set to learn and understand, *not to sell.* And, of course, that mind-set and sincerity came through in our body language, the questions we asked, and the way we asked the questions — we focused on listening intently and proving that by summarizing what he was saying and asking for clarification.

If you are truly focused on taking good notes, you will not be tempted to interrupt or jump in with an answer. And most of the time, the other person will keep talking.

We found out there was an annual bid process in which we could choose to participate but it was all done in a different department (procurement of course). We got the contact details and an endorsed introduction to those contacts. In fairness, this was a county bid so there was an entire process to go through that we later found was not as complex as we had initially feared.

With that information, Joe could decide whether to proceed or not based on the facts and the real value of the opportunity.

Points to Consider and Remember

By now you have certainly figured out that the fundamental principles of Silent Selling and the needs assessment process don't change from scenario to scenario. I put the different examples in hoping that one or more of them will relate to a situation you have dealt with. If you have started to notice these five things, you are right on course:

■ You can use the needs assessment techniques if you are sincere and are really interested in getting more insight and information. In most cases the information will follow.

- It's perfectly OK to admit you don't know something. In fact, to most customers, it is really quite a refreshing change from the traditional sales approach.
- If you can keep customers talking about what matters to them, using the humble and curious approach and summarizing after every few points, you will get most, if not all, of the insight they have about their own organization.
- You can recover from most any situation or get permission to let it go — be humble, admit fault, then ask for permission and, later, advice on how to move forward.
- Silence is one of the most powerful sales tools you have.

One final point, on which we will spend more time in the final chapter — most of the client examples I used involved very experienced sales people. The most senior, most successful, and most talented sales people are the ones who get the most out of using this process. That's partially because they are the best and the brightest. But it also can be attributed to the fact that they have deeply seeded legacy behaviors that needed changing. Sometimes mountains of experience can work against you.

Suggestions for the Sales Person

One approach for conducting the first few needs assessment interviews is to pick three questions that you are comfortable with. After each conversation evaluate how well the questions were received, the caliber of information and insight you were able to get, and especially *how you felt* (amygdala check) during the conversation.

I always remind clients that these are not acting lessons. It's about learning a new skill and you can expect it to feel awkward at first. It is new behavior (that limbic brain again) that takes time to transition and learn. Practice is essential.

After a few trials using your three questions (and perhaps a belly flop or two), assess whether or not you want to stay with the current questions or if you're ready to expand the repertoire. The questions that are most effective for you and your style will evolve over time. Take time to do your own analysis — this is where and when the learning occurs. The review and analysis is how you establish your own style and become effective at this skill. It is a crucial step that will help shape your future as a sales person.

Suggestions for the Manager or Coach

As a sales manager, or someone who is teaching or coaching sales people through this learning process, consider these suggestions as you work with your team:

- Encourage team members to do a couple of "belly flops" on smaller, less complex accounts. They need to:
  - Feel the awkwardness of not having the discussion go as they had hoped.
  - Be reminded that this is a new skill.
  - Understand that this will take time to learn.

Also, encourage them to have a laugh at their own expense — it is a tremendous tension reducer. They must understand that it is OK to not know everything.

In order to take full ownership of teaching the new skills and having the sales person become a regular user, consider that:

- Each person must do this at his or her own pace, in their own way. There is no one way to learn.
- You want to facilitate the sales person actually learning new ways of thinking and filtering information versus managing your expectations — very few people can do both well, especially at the same time. If the sales person is worried about managing the boss's expectations, the chance of actually learning new behaviors is slim.
- Verbally abusing someone, forcing them, or threatening them is a sure-fire technique to ensure that no learning occurs.

Keep the Learning Going

When coaching someone who has a strong emotional investment in a particular set of beliefs that is not supported by empirical data and/or appears to have some flaws in their thinking, you must let them progress at their own rate.

So be smart about setting the emotional tone. If you force it, you could cause someone to become defensive. They won't be able to grasp new skills and can resort to the fight or flight syndrome. The bigger issue is that the next time you are coaching the sales person their amygdala will cue them that an uncomfortable feeling is on the way. Then their brain's ability to learn will shut down again.

This doesn't mean you can't push sometimes. You just don't push *every* time. The decision when to push is a function of the current situation combined with your knowledge of the individual, your experience, and gut instincts. If they refuse to acknowledge new behaviors or learning at some point, then you have to ask yourself a series of questions about this individual's capabilities, which is another problem altogether.

There are a few ways to effectively manage a person's learning curve. You can use all of, part of, or your version of this approach:

- If the individual reports directly to you, influence and manage learning by working on it as a regular part of your coaching and development work.
- Use questions such as, *The last time we worked together, we talked about x, y, or z* (whatever the topics were). *As I recall your perspective was… How have you been thinking about that since then?*
- If they have a good answer, then work with it. If they don't, then you have identified a potential problem.
- Be careful ***not to volunteer*** the answers to your questions. For the best results, coach them through explaining their answer and the rationale behind it in a nurturing and humble fashion. Examples of questions to get this conversation started:
    - *Put on your consultant's hat. What do you think is really going on with this customer, beyond the product issues?*
    - *What do you see here that maybe I am not seeing or understanding thoroughly?*
    - *What is the one question we could ask the customer to get a better read on what is going on inside their organization?*
- If I have only one or two days with someone, I use another version of this same approach:
    - I ask the previous question several times during the day.
    - Or, I ask:

- *My sense is that you have a degree of confidence in that perspective. Do I have that right?*
- *Could you help me understand more about that from your perspective?*
- *Since we haven't worked together before (or very often), what insight could you share with me that would help me understand why that approach feels right to you?*
- *It sounds like it has worked really well for you in the past. Please tell me about some of the situations that it worked really well.*

- Another method is to simply encourage the person to think more about their perspective and ask themselves *what part of their approach is working and what, if any, parts might need re-thinking?*
  - *In the approach we have been using, we are not morally obligated to continue to use it if it is not meeting our expectations. If we start with a blank piece of paper here, what would the approach look like?*
  - *What would the key element be and how would we know if we were successful?*

In this type of conversation, be it with a customer or someone you are coaching, using silence is very important — it is one of your most important and effective tools. Ultimately, the goal is to get them thinking and moving towards the right conclusions. Then it is about them figuring it out and owning it for themselves versus you force feeding it. Sadly, some sales people will simply agree with the manager to get through the discussion and then revert back to the old ways as soon as the manager leaves.

Remember, this is the limbic brain at work here. It takes time and repetition, especially if the goal is to let go of old, legacy behaviors that are no longer effective. When a sales person comes to a conclusion on his or her own, they can then claim ownership of the insights (such as Mary who used her instincts, experience, and intellect versus me persuading her). That's empowering and encourages new learning.

Unfortunately, too few sales managers create a climate of confidence or candor where it's OK to admit you don't know everything. This effectively ends the learning process and wastes time, resources, and especially money.

Chapter 7

The Sales Process

This Isn't Brain Surgery

Let's be clear about this process. This is not brain surgery nor is it complex or new. It is really very simple, straightforward, and easy to use. It does, however, have one characteristic that a health club membership also has. You guessed it right — you have to actually use it to benefit from it!

Undoubtedly you have seen and probably worked with many sales programs or processes in the past. Frankly, what I sometimes struggle with is that some of them don't feel like any sales person actually participated in the development of the content. Most of them feel too "consultant-like."

Most of the programs I have seen have five distinct challenges in one form or another:

- Too much focus on the tactics and the parts — the graphics and the terminology get most of the focus and attention rather than whether or not the process actually helps you sell more effectively.
- There is no process to effectively set priorities or track your progress and most lack any mechanism to share organizational or individual learning from what has worked in the past and what hasn't worked — which is a huge learning opportunity!
- Few of them allow for any consideration of an individual's personality, level of experience, or learning style:
    - They treat the sales person with one year of experience the same as the sales person with 20 years of experience.

- The same direction is provided for calling on the president of a multi-billion dollar company or the owner of a shoe store.
  - There is a wide range of needs, expectations, and business literacy at different levels and the sales approach needs to accommodate for that.
- The sales person has limited to no opportunity to practice the new behaviors on sales calls or using behavior modeling, a learning essential. (You may recall from chapter two that the limbic brain is as much about learning new behaviors as unlearning old habits so repetition and practice are essential.) None of these programs account for that.

Having said all of that, you must have a process. Otherwise you have no way to track what works and what doesn't or how things are changing. The message is you need some type of process — even one that has some flaws is better than none at all. You can use ours (*and it's free, with the purchase of this book, because it's right here, and we aren't going to try to sell you bells and whistles to go along with it! Seriously, you don't need to pay us for an Excel-type tracking system or graphs you could do yourself.*) and customize it to what works for you.

There are other good processes. Just pick one that works for you and your organization.

Our process provides a checklist for all senior executives, sales managers, and heads of sales regarding the development of the professional skills of your sales team. If you are hiring a company to develop the skills of your sales team or have a training department, you must make sure that any skill set development work undertaken includes the following.

Professional Development Program "Must-Haves"

- Clear, concise, well-defined skills and competencies which comprise the elements of the ideal sales skill set and the desired protocol as you define it.
- A solid foundation and fundamentals with enough flexibility so that the process can be customized to each person's style, personality, comfort level, and types of customers with whom each works.

- Fieldwork with each of the sales people, in their market, with their customers — this essential and critical step is one that many companies overlook.
- A mechanism for ongoing feedback and discussion about the process, the calls, what is working, and what is not.
- Reinforcement and updating the tools and best practices which must include sharing success stories and new learning.

Implementing an Improved Sales Process

- You are changing behavior, which is limbic brain – this takes time, repetition, and coaching.
- If the sales process changes are large and complex, you need to *prioritize and implement in phases.*
- It's important to *validate and optimize* each process and program prior to expansion.
- Development team *must include top talent* to ensure the highest probability of success.
  - Over invest in getting the best and the brightest people involved early on because they are the ones who will get the most benefit from learning new skills as the gap between this group and the lesser performers widens.
  - Overall learning for the entire organization will be much greater.
- Deeply involve the Leadership Team.

Use of a Sales Process

I am personally a strong believer in the Silent Selling process because I have been using the fundamental elements for about 15 years and have shared these fundamental elements with any number of clients. Admittedly, I take this position with a high degree of personal bias and emotional equity. This does not mean it is the right one for you or your organization, only you can decide that.

If this particular sales process doesn't work for you, fair enough. You do, however, need to have something to keep your focus, track your learning, and organize your work. So use whatever process will work for you. There are certainly enough of them available and many of you are already working in organizations that have a process. But you must use one of them — consistently. Otherwise, you will have great difficulty tracking your progress, learning, or development.

In terms of which sales process to use, you have three choices: this one, another one, or none at all — which means you will spin your wheels and ultimately waste a lot of time.

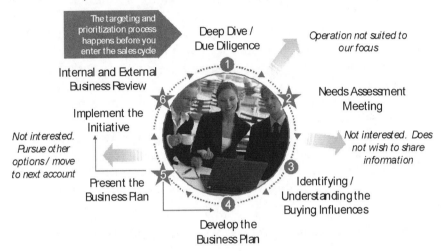

There are seven elements of the sales cycle, including the targeting and prioritization work, and you should notice right away the fact that it is shaped as a circle — which means you should always be somewhere in this process with a customer or a qualified prospect. (The stars signify meetings with the customers. The other points indicate work that you undertake.)

The sales process is comprised of these seven steps:

1. **Targeting & Prioritization:** Setting priorities is a system where you consistently decide where to put your focus. Some elements are must-haves and some you must customize to your own business and the unique characteristics of that business, its maturity, distribution patterns, etc. (you do this before you actually enter the sales process).
   We have found, over time, that when we go back and meet with clients or audit how they are doing, that most clients actually develop a much more effective system of targeting and prioritization as they work with the outline

we started on together. All we did was help them get started in unleashing their internal horsepower.

2. **Pre-Call Protocol:** The work you must do to "earn the right to ask for a meeting with a decision maker."

3. **Needs Assessment Interview:** How to conduct an effective meeting with a qualified prospect or customer. This is the fundamental new behavior to learn and the one that takes the most time.

4. **Identifying & Understanding the Buying Influences:** Who matters and what roles do they play? Which votes count? Whose opinions and authority really matter? How are decisions really made here?

5. **Developing the Plan:** This you can already do using what you have learned in the first four steps.

6. **Presenting the Plan:** Why you are never **not** in the needs assessment mind-set, even if you are making the presentation.

7. **Internal & External Business Review:** Your ticket to get back inside the customer's organization to look for new opportunities.

At Bellwether Food Group, we work with clients on only the first four of these steps. The step we always focus on and talk about in great detail is step three — the needs assessment interview.

Here's why. Of all the steps, the needs assessment interview, the discussion, is the most behavior intensive. If you can do that effectively, consistently, and thoroughly, have good sales instincts, and closely follow the principals introduced here — before, during, and after the presentation — then you will see how all the other elements fit together — the issues, the critical information, the financials, the politics, etc. You will get that insight if you learn the Silent Selling method.

We will work in two aspects of selling that must come *before* you do the presentation:

- **Analysis, Diagnosis, and Planning:** Tools and techniques that focus on learning enough about the customer's business, priorities, culture, and decision-making patterns so that you get the right message to the right buying influences and the most strategically qualified prospects.
- **Execution:** Using these tools combined with your existing talents, skills, experience, style, and personality. This consists of conducting

needs assessment interviews, identifying and understanding the buying influences, setting priorities, and building the business case — all the work that ultimately generates the sale.

You must do both, not one or the other. If you do all the upfront work but don't have developed sales talent to execute, then you simply won't perform as well as someone who does. That is just the reality. Given my physical make up and size, the chances of me ever playing professional football were very unlikely, no matter how hard I may have trained or practiced.

Of course, if you have the sales talent, instincts, contacts, and skill, but don't follow the rigor and discipline of the analysis, diagnosis, and planning, then you will not do as well as someone who has the talent *and* does the work.

The reason for doing all this is so you get smarter about and better at identifying the most likely opportunities for success, using some relatively new learning about the behavioral sciences in your own style and personality. That way, you are more successful.

The goal is that you get smarter about and better at identifying the most likely opportunities for success, using some relatively new learning about the behavioral sciences in your own style and personality.

Most clients find the majority of what we develop and teach falls into one of three categories:

- Informally using at least some of these basic principles in one way or another at some time. All we are really doing here is organizing these principles, techniques, and behaviors into a system so you can get better at working on the right opportunities.
- They have felt that their guts instincts were accurate and that some of these behavioral science principles might be factors but weren't really sure they could be valid, nor sure of how to apply these principles to what they were seeing and learning from customers.
- Pleasantly surprised about how much information is out there, available in the public domain, at no cost, about the customers and prospects.

If you have purchased this book and have read this far, then chances are pretty good that you are already insightful enough and have seriously invested in developing your sales insights, talents, and excellent presentation skills, be they electronic or verbal.

What we are working on is the foundation, so that when you make that really cool, over-the-top presentation with all the fancy stuff, the message is right and resonates with what is really important to those who will actually make the decision to buy.

Common Traits of Successful Sales People

To clarify, these four common traits and competencies of excellent sales people cannot be learned in this or any other book. My belief is that you innately have these four talents/skills and continue to refine them over time:

- Experience
- Industry contacts
- People skills
- Good gut instincts

The successful sales people with whom I have worked and known have had all, or most of, these traits. Some would argue that you are born with the characteristics and talents. I could make a case either way. What is for certain is that you either have them or you don't.

There is one other trait or characteristic that is extremely important for sales and, again, most either have it or don't. You must be genuinely and sincerely interested in and curious about other people and your customers' business. You simply can't fake that. If you are not really interested in the other peoples' business, they eventually sense it.

The most successful sales people tend to be sincerely curious about and interested in their customers' business. This interest and curiosity must be genuine. If it is disingenuous or insincere, the customer will see right through you.

In our workshops, we talk about some very successful people and use three specific examples of individuals whom I personally admire. These three are:

- Celine Dion
- Ringo Starr
- Winston Churchill

Each of them has or had all of these four characteristics or traits:

1. Students of their craft
2. Great collaborators
3. Commitment to learning
4. Excellent planners

Students of Their Craft

One great student of her craft is Celine Dion. While watching a *60 Minutes* report a few years ago, I was not surprised to learn that Celine Dion had a voice coach at the time, even though she was selling more records than anyone.

In that same show, it showed her spending time with a group of gospel singers in Houston. While it was clear to me that she and the other women were having fun, you can bet they were learning from each other as well.

The Great Collaborator

Ringo Starr is not necessarily known as a great drummer. However, his true value to the Beatles was his ability to collaborate with John Lennon and Paul McCartney as they were writing songs.

In a *New Yorker* article in June 2007, McCartney talked about Ringo Starr and George Harrison. He described them as musicians who knew what to do with a song without a lot of direction and, hence, were both great collaborators. McCartney added, *They would just go yeah, yeah. They wouldn't go with what you meant. None of that. Ringo would stand there with his sticks, do a couple of beats. We'd just go to our things and play.*

Excellent Planners

Winston Churchill, many historians believe, is the one person who is responsible for a free Western Europe in the twentieth and twenty-first centuries and the development and growth of the USA before World War II. Had it not been for Churchill and his leadership, the world might look very different today.

One of the most interesting things about Churchill is how many different things he learned to do and do very well. During the Boer

War, he occasionally wrote dispatches for some of the London papers. From that personal experience he learned how that process and business worked.

Commitment to Learning

In another of his roles, Churchill was the head of organizing the British Navy. He learned all about that so when he became prime minister during the war he had a working knowledge of the military overall.

By the time he became prime minister, he had a tremendous grasp of how to communicate with the public, get the right message out, and tell the truth in a way that got the citizens working together. Beyond that, he made it a point to be friends with and kept regular contact with President Franklin Roosevelt, well before Pearl Harbor.

When it came time to make all the tough decisions he had to make as prime minister during World War II he had already studied the navy, the logistics, and understood the mood of the country. This helped in two ways in that he knew what resources were available and did an incredible job of communicating with the British people — all things he had prepared his entire life to do. Oh yes, and he also had established a solid relationship with his most important ally, President Roosevelt.

The point of all this is that the best are always working on improving their skills and talents. They work on rounding out all the skills needed, not just a few!

You Can't Skip Any Steps!

You don't always have to follow these steps in order. You will move around a bit at times and have multiple initiatives within customer organizations where you may be in different steps in the process.

But you must do the work! It's not really difficult or, at least, the majority of it is not complex. Yet the rigor and the discipline of sticking with the system really matters! If you skip steps or cut corners, it will come back to haunt you. It's not unlike the preflight checklist that the pilot goes through before every flight. It isn't complex and can even be a chore — especially on a hot, rainy, or cold day — but it can save your life!

The times I have cut corners, and we are all guilty of that, are the times I have missed things that cost me a client, project, or sale. The steps are not rocket science but you have to follow them!

Okay, enough on that already. You do these so that you get to the truth about an opportunity, the overall situation, or what is going on with the other person sooner rather than later, or not at all.

Going for the "No"

Going for the "no" is a radical departure for most sales people. Whenever I first introduce this concept to clients, especially if it's a senior executive who has been in the position for a long time, I expect, and usually get, a response like, *What are you thinking, Mac? We need our sales people to be positive and focused on driving the business, not looking for ways to not gain business.* There is, at first, a quite similar reaction from the sales people.

Think about this challenge using these questions (You don't want to necessarily share your thoughts with anyone yet):

- Over the last five years, what percentage of the business proposals you made in a one-year period actually sold?
- How many times were there in the last two years, truth be told, when you didn't really feel that good about an opportunity but made the proposal anyway, because you felt pressure to try, even though you knew in your gut, if you allowed yourself to be honest about it, the likelihood was slim?
  - Was it the pressure to have "activity" or an active pipeline?

For more on this subject, check out William Ury's book, *The Power of a Positive No.* It is one of my favorites.

How Customers Make Sales People Go Away

There is a fairly common tactic used by business professionals and many senior executives who are frequently approached by sales people or consultants. It is very simple and my guess is you have all heard it more than once.

I have been told this by many senior executives. The best way to get rid of any sales person or consultant it to say, *Sure, that sounds really interesting. We need to take a look at that, send me a proposal.*

The best way to get rid of any sales person or consultant is the "Sure, that sounds really interesting, we need to take a look at that, send me a proposal" approach. That pretty much works every time." - Rob Hardy, Founding Partner, Bellwether Food Group

Two professionals, whom I know quite well, my business partners at Bellwether Food Group, are not sales people. Jon Jameson was a senior executive at two publicly traded companies (Denny's and Panera Bread) and Rob Hardy was in product development and marketing for Ragu and Campbell's so they both dealt with a lot of sales people.

Both Jon and Rob have told me this was one way of dealing with sales people whom they wanted to go away and was a commonly used tactic — *Just ask them for a proposal. That's the quickest way to get a sales person or a consultant out of your office or off the phone.*

Real World Application

This doesn't mean you don't do proposals in situations that aren't perfectly defined — that simply doesn't exist. Of course you do. What this does mean is that you can truly be more productive by not investing in that 20-30 percent of proposals that maybe won't go anywhere, at least not for you.

On the subject of blind Request for Proposals (RFPs), I ask three basic questions:

- Is it possible for you to set up a conversation with a senior level decision maker to have a needs assessment discussion either over the phone or in person?
- What has been your experience in doing business with this organization in the past?
- How much do you know about this customer's business and how it's doing?

For me, there can be at least two immediate warning signs:

- ***They won't talk about their business:*** If the business proposal is not important enough to the prospective customer that they don't want to make sure their suppliers understand their business and strategy and won't make anyone available to meet with someone, that is a major red flag.
- ***You are guessing:*** If you have never worked with the company and don't know much or anything about how they make decisions, that's a yellow flag.

Many times, these buying decisions are already, or close to, being made. This alleged RFP work is either a formality or one of two other things:

- A "CYA": The company, usually one that is publicly traded, needs a paper trail of multiple bids for a fallback position or in case of some type of audit. It may also be political, so that if someone starts to ask difficult questions later on, those with the responsibility have a paper trail. The recent new rules, such as in Sarbanes-Oxley, have made this even worse.
- An exercise that justifies the existence of certain internal staff — Purchasing, Quality Assurance, and others. Proceed at your own risk.

Remember, there is one resource you have exactly the same amount of as everyone else on the earth, including your competitors — time. Spend it wisely!

Time — the one resource you have exactly the same amount of as everyone else on the earth, including your competitors. Spend it wisely!

Inaction — The Hidden Competitor

Interestingly, my experience in consulting has been that your primary competition is not another firm but inaction. Often times, there is political pressure to "look at things differently" or, in the case of selling products or services business to business, to "evaluate our supplier relationships." They may or may not be serious about changing but the activity starts in earnest none the less. That is, the client goes through a series of machinations, yet ultimately doesn't do the work or they do it "internally" — which is basically the same thing as agreeing to stay with the status quo.

Following are some of the patterns you will see, some common ways customers behave, and some suggestions on how you might, at least, get a better understanding of what is really happening and perhaps how to handle them.

First, to understand why clients and customers will go through an exercise like this, I asked about 20 senior executives (presidents and vice presidents) from the foodservice industry, primarily manufacturers and chain restaurants. The reasons they listed:

- Change of direction in their organization.
- After working on it and talking about it internally, it was "put on the back burner." I probed that further and found this usually meant that the strong political players in their organization either didn't support it or changed their position.
  - Another way to think about it is management teams, like individuals, sometimes confuse talking about an issue or a vendor with actually doing something differently about or with an issue or a vendor. They are two very different things.
  - You see this sometimes with people who need to lose weight, drink less, work harder, get organized, etc. They will go through a venting process which essentially gives them permission to talk about something they're not happy about.
  - For many, that venting process makes them feel better for at least a short time and because they have talked about it, the pressure to make changes becomes less intense (If you have ever known an alcoholic, they are really good at this).
  - The harsh reality is that nothing changes but at least temporarily they have been able to let off some steam.
- They value the relationship with the vendor or the person for any number of reasons — this person is a good person to know, a good source of information, someone who may help in a job search, or they may genuinely enjoy talking with the sales person.

How These Patterns Impact Sales Effectiveness

It is not unlike what happens when sales people are inundated with reports — driven by the need for internal data, they focus on getting the reports done and become good at getting the right information to those who demand it. As a result you get:

- Reports rather than getting smarter about what's important to customers, their business, their industry, and the things that move the business forward.
- The reports will rarely make a sales person more effective, although the exercise might force them to think more thoroughly. It mostly makes them more proficient at completing the reports, not making sales or managing relationships. The last time I checked, reports don't generate revenue. If sales performance isn't where it needs to be, increasing reports will not fix that.
- If the reports are intended as inspection devices, then that is what you will get — inspection-driven information. This information will come to you in a fashion and format intended to get the inspection over with as soon as possible.

Worse, if there is a culture of always only giving the right answer, then you will eventually be in trouble, for a number of reasons:

- If sales people are given incentives to give only the right answer, or disincentives for candor, they will respond to whatever incentives are put in place.
- Sales people will also model the behavior and emotional tone of the leadership team and the management with whom they deal.
- That tone, attitude, and behavior will be evident in front of the customers.
  - Best examples: Starbucks, Southwest Airlines, FedEx, Nordstrom

What will make a sales person more effective are these things:

- Working on what matters to customers and the implications.
- Understanding what is going on with customers, why it is going on, and what, if anything, your firm can do to influence that.
- Consistently working on their professional skills.
- Setting priorities.
- Listening!!!

Becoming more effective at Silent Selling takes so long because we are generally not very good listeners. In our culture, listening as a skill is undervalued.

You certainly have noticed, and may even agree with me, that the American culture does not put a premium on listening. Our cultural bias is to offer quick solutions that sound compelling or clever, regardless of how well these solutions might work. Typically, we measure the outputs and final results and pay scant attention to the details of how progress is actually made or what steps actually need to be taken to get the desired results.

One evening watching the cable and network news shows is enough to prove this point. What you see during any political campaign season is a great example. Each of the candidates has philosophies, theories, beliefs, and plans for action. Yet none of them, of any political persuasion, will set up valid metrics or success thresholds. If these candidates were put into the for-profit world and attempted to use the strategies some of these candidates use lacking solid data, with nonexistent performance thresholds, against poorly defined goals, they would not last very long!

It's all about the talking heads trying to sound more clever, more experienced (whatever *that* means), and more compelling than the competition. When is the last time you noticed any of them really listening?

There is one talk show professional who is a great listener, who has an amazing, incredible, emotional intelligence, and talent for connecting with anyone. The best I have ever seen in my life is Oprah Winfrey. Watching her is like watching a great dancer or talented athlete work. She makes it look so easy. She is brilliant. I don't know the woman but I am pretty confident that she works at that regularly.

The Old School Must be Retired

In sales, for many years, the common wisdom was that you made or lost a sale at the end, which of course meant the focus was on "closing skills." This is about the sales person "persuading" the customer to buy. If you ever try that approach with a senior executive, business owner, or purchasing manager, you'll get told to go away or thrown out of their office pretty quickly — as you should be!

If you are selling automobiles, then perhaps that approach works, but not if you are a true professional in the business world, especially if you are in the banking, software, food, beverage, or foodservice industry today. This approach is a recipe for failure.

If you have been in sales for very long, in a business-to-business role, you know that trying to persuade someone to purchase something they don't need is a waste of time.

The fact remains that if you don't get a sale in 80 percent or better of the cases, you missed something early in the process or simply didn't ask enough questions. At this point in a workshop, I am usually asked, *What do I do if they won't answer or don't know.* The fact that they won't say or don't know speaks volumes about whether or not you can help them or whether they have the ability to actually buy anything. To be sure, it's not the answer you wanted, but it is legitimate, admittedly painful, feedback.

The other part of that answer is that the only ones who ever ask that are those who have never tried the Silent Selling approach.

Why It Takes Time to Get to the Real Truth

There are five reasons it takes some time to get the true, real-life story from almost everyone and the first reason is the most important:

1. In most cases, the other person doesn't really believe that you, or most anyone else, are really going to listen and invest in understanding why this subject or issue matters to them at this time. When we are asked questions, too many times we give a quick answer, rather than one we have thought through.
2. What this means to you if you are a sales person is that you often-times provide an answer to a business issue that is simply not well thought out.
3. To accurately or effectively understand and then communicate what is on their mind, about 15-20 percent of the people you will talk to are not used to having anyone really listen to them.
4. They haven't had the time or really worked on thinking their challenges or specific issues through in enough detail, beyond the symptoms.
5. The most common reason is *you* have another agenda. *You* want them to behave in a certain way, agree to or endorse something they don't really believe in, understand, or want to do, or you are trying to sell them something they either don't want or aren't qualified to buy!

This last pattern is very evident in two places today — the business world, specifically in sales, and in our personal lives with someone we are close to, be it a spouse, lover, sibling, child, parent, or close friend.

There are two factors working together here, the first driving at least part of the second:

- Your body language, tone of voice, and facial expressions send the message that you aren't listening *and...*
- The other person immediately senses this so you lose any chance of a sincere, truthful conversation because they feel the pressure and the tension in some cases.

We have all been on the receiving and sending side of this type of discussion. We're all probably more likely and sensitive to having felt this way when others have talked to us. Just as you did in that situation, the other person can sense that you are not fully engaged in listening, even if they don't say it. So the other person starts to work on getting rid of their own awkwardness rather than focusing on the real issues.

Let's take a look at these examples to dive into what really happens in these discussions, define the issues, and understand the patterns, including why we behave our way into a less-than-desirable situation.

Silent Selling is a proven process, an example of how to get to the truth by looking at what we might typically do and then look at one way to handle it. You can use this approach for a misunderstanding with a spouse, with a customer you don't currently do business with, or with a customer who you have been doing business with for a while but are not sure how it's really going.

For the sake of this example, let's assume you are already seated in their office, in your home, or wherever and have established these three goals for the meeting:

1. Begin to establish a professional or better dialogue with this individual.
2. Learn about the company's goals or this person's goals/ expectations.
3. Learn more about how they make decisions.

According to the purchasing and product development executives I interviewed for the book (sales people indicate similar patterns) and my own experience in many personal relationships, the old-fashioned, traditional way goes something like this:

- Introduction.
- Explanation of why you're there/why you are talking about this now.
- Introduction of service or product or what you want to happen.
- Presentation about your company and products, your wishes, your opinion.
- The other person pushes back with a version of: price/We are happy with our current supplier./We aren't looking at that right now./ That's not want I want./That's not fair to me. (Pick one.)
- Trial close for next steps — you then work on either persuading or gaining agreement.

Then you, as the sales person or the person who wants something, does over 50 percent of the talking because you have to get everything out that the customer needs to know about new products, or something else that the customer doesn't care about and isn't relevant to what they are working on at the time. In a personal situation, it is typically, *Well, if I just explain it to them, tell them how important this is to me, or push hard enough, it will go my way.*

Ultimately, you leave the meeting or end the discussion hoping the person may eventually buy something, give in, see it partially your way, or at least give you an appointment the next time you are in town making calls with your boss.

Let's look at a better way. For the sake of this example, we'll assume that you are prepared to demonstrate to this stranger, your close friend, or family member that you have made a sincere effort to learn something new about them or their business. We'll assume that if you bought this book, you are serious enough about your role as a sales professional to realize this is important and that the customer or prospect knows immediately if you have done your homework or not — and if you are truly willing to listen or not.

If you haven't done this step, then you are destined to fail. In the final analysis, you already know why this — sounding informed and showing the prospective customer you take them seriously — is important and increases your chances of selling something — all legitimate reasons for doing the pre-call work.

There is one other, really important, fundamental reason you do the learning and work before the meeting:

- It impacts how you feel when go into the meeting.
- You have done the learning, legwork, planning, and research before the first meeting with a prospective customer *because...*
- ...it impacts your frame of mind, attitude, and comfort level, *so that...*
- ...you are more relaxed and comfortable and in the state of mind to have an adult-to-adult business discussion with this person *and...*
- ...you don't have to act like a sales person.

Instead of sounding like a sales person, you sound like a peer or someone who has at least begun to understand the other person's business or point of view and why it is important to them. In my view, that is something that makes you stand out.

Chapter 8

Summary and Getting Started

As we wrap up here, let me state one thing clearly — to get the value out of this book, you have to use it!

So what I suggest is two things.

First, use this book as a reference. Carry it in your briefcase or handbag — it should fit. Highlight the relevant points that work for you and make copies of whatever parts you need and use them for personal use.

Next, make the principles fit your style and personality as well as the industry and organizational culture you work in, which should be very doable. This process and these tools are *to serve you* — not the other way around — so tweak and *customize them to work for you.* Simply stick to the principle of open-ended questions — that is questions that cannot be answered with a simple yes or no.

Pick Your Favorite Questions

When you are just getting started, pick 3-4 questions that you like and use them over the course of a couple of weeks to see how they work for you. You will find that your own preferences and what works for your style will become apparent to you fairly quickly.

One key thing to keep in mind is that you can use fewer words in the questions than you think are necessary. One of the mistakes many people make at first is to make the questions too long or to suggest part of the answer in the question. You don't want to do that because you want the other person to take you wherever the conversation needs to go. So let that happen.

Again, this just takes two things — being sensitive to the words you are actually using and working to get the message across with fewer words.

See How Much Information You Can Get

One great way to have some fun while learning is to try to get as much information from the other person as you can without them asking you anything about you. This is much easier than you think it is going to be.

Start the conversation off with a wide-ranging question about them, their life, or how they got to be working where they work or living where they live. You will be surprised at how much they will reveal if you show real interest and then let them talk.

The idea is to work to gain proficiency at drawing other people out. That is how you get very good at conducting needs assessment interviews and getting the information, insights, and context most people never get. This is the hidden secret of successful selling today — getting the insights, perspective, and access to the people other sales people never will. Those sales people are selling their products or services as unique but Silent Sellers are in another league.

My own personal record is about one hour and thirty minutes with a complete stranger. In more than a few situations, this process has provided more information and insight than I had ever imagined and, in a few cases, more than I wanted! But the point is, the approach works more often than not.

Practice in a Safe Environment

Practice in your daily life, at the store, the drycleaners, school, local bar, health club, church/synagogue/mosque, wherever. Most people will be flattered that you are actually interested and you will see the three phases — sincerity, venting, truth.

Be mindful that some won't engage right away and may take longer to open up. Of course, there are those who will never open up but the vast majority of people will.

As I mentioned before, use this approach with a loved one or someone close to you. It will be very interesting for all concerned.

Cheat!

Cheating is strongly encouraged. For example, write the questions down on cards or a notepad and take them into the meeting with you. If you are uncomfortable doing that, try telling the other person something like, *I apologize for this but I wanted to make sure I didn't forget to ask you any of the questions I had been thinking about, so I hope you don't mind that I printed them out in preparation for our discussion today.*

You can absolutely take a list of questions into any meeting with you and feel free to use them as your guide. There is absolutely no reason you can't do this. At the very least, it sends a message to the other person that you take the meeting very seriously and spent the time to prepare.

Of course, you can always take notes and ask for clarification and more detail as you do that during the meeting. It is perfectly fine and most people will really appreciate it.

Silence: The Secret Weapon

And finally — use the silence! Let the customers talk. They will tell you everything you need to know. Just let them do it.

So yes, go into your next sales call with only a notepad, a pen, and your business cards — no brochures, no jokes, and no widgets — and see how it works. You will be pleasantly surprised! Make the call all about the customer and they will probably reward you with new and compelling insights.

Finally, I hope this is helpful to you and makes you more successful at whatever you love to do professionally. I am very open to learning about your experiences and hearing whatever feedback would be helpful to you or our clients so do let me hear from you.

If you have questions, comments, ideas, or an interesting sales scenario you want to talk about or share, please contact me at: mbrand@bellwetherfoodgroup.com

Good luck!